ACTING DAFT

(IT'S NEVER TOO LATE FOR CHANGING)

Amanda Maclachlan

Amanda Maclachlan

Published by
Chipmunkapublishing
PO Box 6872
Brentwood
Essex CM13 1ZT
United Kingdom

http://www.chipmunkapublishing.com

Chipmunkapublishing gratefully acknowledges the support of Arts Council England.

ACTING DAFT

Chapter One: The early years

It was a hot summer day in the middle of August. Fairy dust fell off the cow slips, casting a silvery glint across the green grass. Mrs Dora Plantington looked briefly out of the window at a grasshopper rasping its legs on a large leaf outside the window. She looked nervously at the counter on the wall. How long was this going to take? The number '3' hung under the name of Doctor Hanson on the white clinical wall of the surgery. Dora looked at the number that was clenched in her hand. It was number five. That meant there were two people before her. Her palm was sweating with nerves. She knew what everyone was thinking; that she was an unfit mother. She tried her best, but the twins where becoming more and more uncontrollable.

The year was 1965. She was dressed in a minidress with big orange flowers on it and had her blonde hair up in a beehive style. Her makeup was perfect and she had false eyelashes that where in fashion. Dora liked to keep herself nice for her husband, despite it getting more difficult to find time for herself now with four children. She watched as her two twin children ran round the surgery whooping and making noises. They were five years old and hadn't started to speak properly yet. They had started to speak in their early years but all of a sudden they had gone silent. It seemed to happen about the same time that Sarah was born. Mrs Plantington was too embarrassed by her children's behaviour to look at anybody — she didn't know what to do except sit quietly, not looking at anybody and pretending they where not hers. Her other two kids where perfectly well behaved. She didn't treat then any differently to the other two as far as she had noticed.

'If they where my kids I'd spank them. Wouldn't you?' commented an elderly man to no one in particular. He was sat behind her in a tweed suit with a boater hat perched precariously on his head, and was holding a walking stick with both hands clenched over a horse's head handle. He scowled at Henry and Winston. As if they would notice when they were too preoccupied with gaining everybody's attention anyway. They loved putting on a show and playing up to an audience.

Dora didn't believe in hitting children. Anyway, she was sure that if she did spank them somebody else would have something to say about it. Whatever one did with the twins, someone always had something to say. Some nasty comment or unhelpful suggestion. She got up off her chair and went running after them, grabbing one of each of their hands and dragging them back to her seats. 'Be good,' she said to them as she pulled them both onto her knee. She looked down on their angelic faces, blonde hair and beautiful blue eyes and softly pulled at Winston's fringe. Then she looked at Harry and ruffled his hair. It was hard to think to look at them they could be so much trouble. Much as they caused her so much embarrassment and pain, she adored them. Her love knew no bounds. They where like little miniatures of her darling husband. She noticed the light was on for Dr Hanson. It was her turn to go in.

'Doctor,' she said, 'as I've told you before, there's something wrong with the twins. They're terribly difficult and they haven't started to speak yet. They did start speaking then they stopped soon after Sarah was born.'

'My diagnosis is the same,' said the doctor. 'Non-specific mental handicap. Dora, you're looking weary. Won't you consider putting them into an institution, and then you can concentrate on your other two children? As you said, they're terribly difficult and you are looking tired.'

'No, definitely not,' said Dora defiantly. 'I'm certainly not putting my kids in a big hospital and forgetting about them. I'm sure they're bright. They're just not very well at the moment. I want them cured — not sending away. They did start to speak when they where little but then they stopped all of a sudden.'

'I'm afraid there is nothing I can do,' said Dr Hanson. 'I can arrange short-term care for them so you can have a rest.'

'I want a second opinion,' she said.

'Any other doctor will only say the same thing as me,' said the exasperated Doctor.

'Then I'll pay private,' she snapped. Dora scooped up the boys, one in each arm, and went back out onto the car park and strapped them into the back seat of her Land Rover. She had paid a fortune to have special seat belts fitted for the twins because it was dangerous driving with them distracting her by bouncing about all over the place. She was upset. She wasn't putting her kids into care. There was something about them; both had a bright, intelligent glint in their eyes. Their cheeky grins. The way they interacted with each other. She knew neither of them where stupid, yet there *was* something wrong. She didn't know what to think. There had to be a cure, something with which to unlock the twins' minds. She wanted the doctors to help them, not lock them up. She was sure something could be done. She just didn't know what.

The twins side glanced at each other then looked at the floor, both with sombre expressions on their faces. For once they sat quietly on the back seat, not moving.

That had been a bit scary — the doctor suggesting having them put in hospital. Still, they knew mummy loved them. They hoped she wouldn't let that happen.

Eventually, she pulled up outside the riding school she owned with her husband and took the twins into the old stone farmhouse.

She had written away to an early learning centre and bought some flash cards. They had pictures with words underneath. She sat the twins down in the lounge and got the cards out. The twins were always well behaved and attentive when she did anything educational with them, but she just didn't get a response.

'House,' she said, pointing to the word for house.

'Baby,' she continued.

The twins watched, fascinated. They were taking everything in and learning to read the words from flash cards and books that their mother read to them. They just weren't interested in speaking to anyone else but each other. They had a bond so strong it was almost telepathic. The twins were extremely intelligent and picked up everything their mother taught them very quickly indeed. They just refused to communicate with anybody else but each other and they only spoke when nobody was listening. If they did speak in front of other people, they spoke in gobble-de-gook that only they could understand. 'Mmm' meant they liked something. 'Ooorrgh' meant they didn't like something or they were angry. They had also begun to develop some secret hand signals. To the onlooker, it seemed as if they where just wriggling their fingers in front of their faces. In fact, they were secret hand signals. Each wriggle of the fingers had a different meaning. They had worked the hand signals out between them at night in bed when the rest of the house was asleep and Dad was snoring loudly from drinking too much whisky. As it happened, they could speak perfectly. They just didn't like other people knowing what they were saying. They spoke in whispered tones when nobody was about to overhear or in their special sign language when people were around. What Henry and Winston wanted to say to each other was nobody else's business as far as they where concerned. They very rarely felt the need to converse with any other members of the family. Besides, keeping dumb suited their purposes. They had found they could act up and get away with it better if Mum and Dad felt that there was something wrong with them — much to their delight and John, their older brother's, horror. He was always getting told off.

John often thought to himself that the twins could murder one of the horses and Mum would just sigh and say nothing much to either of them. Sarah was too young to notice. She had never known anything different, unlike John who had his parents' undivided attention until the twins where born. Now, it was like he didn't exist anymore unless he did something wrong; in which case, Mum came down on him like a ton of bricks. At one time, if he brought a picture home from school Mum would pore over it for ages. 'I can see that's a horse,' she would say enthusiastically. 'Is that me? Oh, how lovely, what a pretty colour my dress is. Oh look, you've drawn a bird. What kind of bird is it John?'

Now when he brought her stuff from school she just glanced briefly at it saying, 'That's nice dear,' then throw it on the table.

Eventually, Dora finished with the flash cards and went to make the evening meal. The nanny knocked on the door and came inside, 'We've been to feed the ducks,' she said, sitting down at the table. It was the first time Dora had hired a nanny. She brought John up on her own and looked after the twins when they were babies. However, she'd got pregnant again by accident and didn't see how she could possibly have coped on her own. The nanny was a godsend. She looked after baby Sarah mainly but she helped out with the housework and the ironing. She sat chatting with her in the kitchen as she helped Dora peel the vegetables.

Henry and Winston took the flash cards out of the box and started reading from them. 'Apple, Orange, Chair, Cup, Plate.' They knew Mother couldn't hear them in the kitchen. Then Harry got a story book from the shelf and started reading it to Winston.

'The Three Billy Goats Gruff,' he whispered.

When Mum came in with a drink, he pretended to be looking at the pictures and turned the book upside down.

So it continued as they grew. They found that if they pretended to be daft they didn't get in so much trouble — people just looked at them exasperated.

They started at special school. Dora had wanted them to go to a normal school but they wouldn't take them in. They said they hadn't enough staff to deal with them. They did basic cooking like how to make a sandwich and cornflake cakes with teacher. Winston and Harry were always very good when the teachers were teaching them something. It was when they got bored that they got into mischief. Then they'd start making a mess. Once they ripped a huge picture off the wall. It had taken the other kids ages to make. They didn't really have any friends at special school. Most of the class disliked them as they where always demanding attention, although sometimes they would make the children laugh with some of their antics. Once, Harry during cooking threw his packet of cornflakes at the teacher and the class was in uproar. He'd grown tired of making cornflake cakes.

Harry and Winston particularly enjoyed music class. They liked making lots of noise playing the tambourine or the triangle or sometimes the tom-tom drums.

When they got home on the special bus, Mum let them go into the front room whilst she went into the kitchen to make the evening meal. They got the astronomy books off the book shelf and started reading them.

'I wish we had a telescope so we could see the rings of Saturn,' whispered Winston.

'Me too,' whispered Harry.

John, their older brother, came home from school and they went very quiet; looking at the pictures and pretending that was all they could do. Sarah was in the kitchen in her high chair. The nanny had gone out as it was her evening off. The twins where jealous of any attention Mrs Plantington gave to John or Sarah as they craved to be the centre of attention and would do anything to make people look at them or provoke a response.

Winston made a hand signal to Harry that meant he was going to do something naughty, and then he got the newspaper off the chair and started tearing it into tiny pieces — making mosaics on the floor with Harry.

'Mum!' shouted John. 'The twins have got the newspaper again.'

Mother came rushing in. 'Oh dear,' she said,

picking the pieces up and throwing them in the bin. 'That's naughty. I've told you before that's naughty. Don't do that again.'

The twins started wriggling their fingers in front of their faces and making funny noises.

'That John spoiling our fun again,' signalled Winston.

'Yes, but we're cleverer than him, we don't get into trouble,' signalled Harry back. 'Mum doesn't shout at us like she'd shout at John if he did it.'

They smiled at each other, knowingly.

'Oh dear,' said Dora exasperated as she went back into the kitchen. She had no idea what to do with the twins when they where naughty. With John, she stopped his pocket money or made him stay in. However, the twins didn't get pocket money and didn't go out with their friends anyway. They didn't need any other friends because, or so they thought, they had each other. Two peas in a pod encased together, entwined, interlocked, and never to be parted from each other.

The nanny had tried putting them in a naughty corner but they'd just ripped the wallpaper off the wall where they'd been sitting and then just made laughing sounds as if they where enjoying the attention. Even the nanny couldn't think of a way to discipline them. They did like playing with toys but it didn't seem to worry the twins unduly if the nanny took the toys out of their bedroom. They seemed to like taking their toys to pieces, so they were soon broken anyway. They were curious about how things had been put together and how things work. The nanny, too, had given up, telling Dora that she wasn't really trained to deal with children with learning difficulties. Still, she was a godsend looking after Sarah and helping with the housework. Especially the ironing.

Dora hated ironing.

John pulled his face. He'd get into big trouble if he did anything like that. The twins always got away with everything, he thought. Mum had no time for him either these days, what with the twins and baby Sarah. Then there was the animal hospital. Dora had trained to be a vet before she gave it up to marry Ted. She had helped him with the stables until John was born. When she gave up work to look after the children, she still found time to take in little woodland creatures that had been brought to her by local people and nurse them back to health before releasing them back into the wild. It had always been her hobby since she gave up her veterinary practice.

Mother called them into dinner. They sat round the big oak dining table. It was Shepherd's pie with steamed cabbage and beetroot. Ted, their father, had come in from the stables and sat at the head of the table. They all tucked in heartily. Winston and Harry could use a spoon but they both started using their fingers instead. They just liked provoking a response and making a mess. The rest of the family ignored them as they had long since given up trying to get them to use cutlery and behave at the dinner table.

'John, take your elbows off the table,' said Dad.

'What?' said John. 'But look at the twins. Look at what the twins are doing Dad, eh, look at the twins. Why do you get at me all the time? You never tell them off for anything.'

'Don't speak to me like that!' scolded Ted. 'The twins can't help it. You can.'

The twins showed no outward reaction, but inside their heads they were laughing. It was funny, they thought, how they could get away with all sorts of things just through acting daft when John couldn't. Harry lunged for the brown sauce and started to drink it out of the bottle. It tasted horrible but he loved the reaction he got.

'Harry, stop it,' said Mother, jumping up. 'You'll make yourself sick,' she said, taking it off him.

'See, look what Harry's doing now Dad,' said John, 'and I get done for putting my elbows on the table. It's not fair, it really isn't.'

'I've told you before!' shouted Dad. 'The twins are special. They can't help it. You can.'

The twins laughed to themselves again in their heads.

'That was funny,' signalled Winston.

'Mum cares,' signed Harry with his fingers, 'whether I make myself sick or not.'

Winston grinned and started making mmm mmm noises to indicate he was enjoying his food. Sarah sat in her high chair eating her Shepherd's pie with a spoon. She was making much less mess than the twins, even at the tender age of two,

When dinner was over, Dad went into the front room, 'Where's my paper?' he said. 'I haven't done the crossword yet.'

'The twins have had it,' said Dora apologetically.

'God damn it. I haven't done the crossword yet,' he said.

'You shouldn't leave it lying about. You know what the twins are like,' said Mother.

'Yes, Yes, I know,' he said, sighing and taking a drink of his tea. Secretly he wished Dora would do what the doctor said and put them in care, but he loved his wife so much he didn't want to upset her by mentioning it. He knew she adored them so much because they looked so much like him. However, they certainly didn't act like him. He hated having to tell John off so much when the twins got away with everything. The thing was he wanted John to turn out decent like himself. He couldn't have John copying off the twins and descending to their level of behaviour.

'I'd get done if I did that,' said John under his breath.

'Yes you would,' said Dad. 'You should know better.'

'See,' signed Winston, 'John would get done but we don't, do we?'

Harry smiled.

When Ted had finished his tea, he went back out to the stables for his evening riding classes. Mother had all the children painting at the kitchen table. Then it was time for bed. She took Sarah up for her bath first and then the twins. John stayed up for a bit as he was the eldest.

'That was funny with the sauce bottle,' whispered Winston. 'Did you see John's face?'

'We're cleverer than John,' said Harry. 'We know how not to get in trouble.'

'Yes,' said Winston. 'John would get dragged over the coals if he did something like that.'

'Goodnight Winston,' said Harry.

'Goodnight Harry,' said Winston, and they both drifted off to sleep.

When Ted came in after the evening session of horse riding classes, Dora went out to see to her woodland creatures. She tended to them during the day when the kids were at school and then checked on them at night. She had a hedgehog with a broken leg and a seagull with a broken wing. She got some herbal potions out of her bag and put some in their water dishes, fed them and then came back to the house. Sometimes, one of John's little friends would come round to help her. He was her prodigy — much more interested in the animals than her own children — and sometimes he would help her release them back into the wild. Little Rodney was an orphan that John had brought home to tea once. He was intensely interested in what she was doing and wanted to learn all the time what to do and how to help her. He already knew the names of all the different herbs she used so he could fetch them for her. His big, soulful eyes were full of compassion as he helped her with the wounded animals. His face would light up with joy as he let them out into the wild. She didn't like to admit it, but she felt more for the child than her own brood. John was just horse mad like his dad and was already showing signs of being as financially minded and profit orientated. Ted knew it was illegal, but he was already letting him put small bets on at the bookies out of his pocket money. He put the bets on for him of course. The twins where beautiful and handsome like their dad, but a handful, and Sarah, well, she was still a baby. Dora always gave Rodney fifty pence pocket money for helping her. She was hoping he would come tomorrow. The hedgehog was ready to be released and she liked having somebody with her when she liberated them back into the wild.

She finished feeding the animals and went back into the house.

'Darling,' she said, coming into the sitting room and sitting on the couch. 'I'm sure sometimes I can hear the twins whispering and stuff when I'm in the kitchen. Then as soon as I pop my head round the door they go quiet. I'm sure they're a lot more intelligent than they're letting on you know. I wish I knew what was wrong with them.'

'You're imagining it love,' said Mr Plantington. 'You're working too hard. God knows I realise you want for them lads to be normal, but they're not and they never will be.'

'They're all there with their cough drops, if we just could find the key to unlock them with,' said Mrs Plantington. 'Maybe a private doctor could help them.'

'Forget it,' he said. 'Love, there's nothing anybody can do. Not even a private doctor and I'm not wasting our money. You paid for one once and he said exactly the same thing as Doctor Hanson.'

'Yes, I suppose you're right dear,' she said.

'Whisky dear?' he asked, walking over to a drinks globe.

'Yes please,' said Mrs Plantington.

'If you ask me, thosc lads are lucky to have a mother like you who's prepared to look after them at home. A lot of mothers would have had them placed in an institution. You're doing everything you can for them Dora. No one could do any more.' He handed her a crystal whisky glass containing ten-year-old Glenmorangie.

'I suppose you're right dear,' she said, sipping her whisky. 'I just have a dream that one day they'll wake up and they'll be normal. They'll be able to help in the stables.'

'It's just a dream,' said Mr Plantington.

The next morning, Mrs Plantington was busy getting everyone up for school. John got himself dressed and walked to the end of the drive to catch the school bus. She got the twins up first so they would be ready for their school bus. She gave them some breakfast — toast and warm milk so they didn't make too much mess. Mr Plantington kept them amused with an old leather wallet he bought on his honeymoon in Blackpool. He didn't use it anymore, but it was a trick one with a special compartment that made things placed inside it disappear from view. The twins loved the smell of the leather and kept holding it in front of their faces to sniff. Mrs Plantington came down the stairs with Sarah ready-dressed and the bus came to pick up the twins for special school. A jolly looking man with a red face and huge smile knocked on the door with his clenched fist. 'Are the twins ready?' he asked. The twins dutifully followed him and got on the bus in their usual seats and grinned as he fastened them into their special harness seat belts. Then Dora put Sarah in her high chair and gave her a bowl of cereal.

'Bye love,' said Ted, giving her a kiss before setting off to the stables.

Chapter Two: The Terrible Teens

The twins had turned eleven years old. It was Monday evening — the twins' horse riding night. Mother led one horse and John the other, with little Sarah skipping merrily along beside them. Sarah had a pony and went riding with her father and John later in the evening. John and Sarah now helped out in the stables every evening when they got home from school, helping to muck out and groom the horses. Sarah loved putting her horse's tail in plaits. John was becoming quite an accomplished rider and had started going with his granddad to show jumping competitions. Sarah wasn't quite as competitive.

Dora thought of the twins. It was the one time they looked at peace with the world; gently bobbing up and down in the saddles. It was like the horses got through to the twins in a way no one else could. They loved riding the horses and would never do anything daft or silly during these sessions. For one thing, they knew that if they did, the horses might throw them off the saddle. For two, they just loved riding. They liked being at one with the horse and communing with nature. They loved the feel of the soft breeze against their faces. They loved the smell of hay and horse sweat. They loved their family as well but it had now just become a way of life to wind them up and exclude them from their own little world. The twins didn't act normal, but then it was of some annoyance to them when people treated them differently, which prompted them to act even dafter and wind people up even more. Their behaviour perpetuated itself like an ever-increasing circle.

When the session was over, Dora took the twins

back to the house whilst Dad, John and Sarah went riding together. Sarah now had her own little pony and John had a dapple-grey stallion. Both animals were also used in the stables for classes. Sarah loved sharing her pony with the other little girls and helping them to climb on her back and showing off that it was really her pony. 'It's my pony,' she would say, 'but I'll let you ride it because you're nice and I like you.'

John, on the other hand, hated having to share his stallion. He was insanely jealous, especially if someone riding it was better and more accomplished than he was which, admittedly, was very rare. Sometimes he would storm off back to his bedroom and stare at the rider galloping over the fields on his horse, nearly insane with jealous hatred. Father had told him it was supposed to be his horse so he didn't see why he should have to share it with the punters.

Dora got the maths books out when she got back and explained the numbers and figures to the twins. She had all the books from the national curriculum and went through things with the twins every night. She had wanted them to go to a normal school, but since her requests had been refused she had decided she'd have to teach them from home. She was sure that one day they would snap out of whatever was wrong with them. She hoped some of the stuff she was teaching them was sinking in. Then she got out Shakespeare's works and read one of the plays to them, letting them see the book so they could see the words as she was reading it. The twins sat quietly and attentively, taking everything in.

Dora left the twins alone in the front room whilst she made supper. She knew her family would be hungry when they came back in. She made her special country soup. It was a vegetable soup made to her own secret recipe. Meanwhile, in the front room the twins had found Sarah's pony magazine. They ripped it into pieces and started making mosaics on the floor.

Eventually, Ted and the children came back in from a hard evening's work. Sarah went into the front room to see the mess they had made with her favourite publication.

'Mummy, Dad, the twins have ripped up my pony magazine again!' she wailed.

'You should know not to leave it lying about,' said Mrs Plantington.

'Oh, they never get done for anything,' she wailed. 'It's not fair.'

'You know they can't help it,' said Dad.

'That upset her,' signalled Harry.

'Yes, serves her right for hogging Mum all the time,' signalled Winston.

They all sat round the table for Mrs Plantington's delicious country soup. This time, the twins used their spoons, although they did finish off by slurping the last bits straight out of the bowl. Mr Plantington went to the toilet to discover one of the twins had blocked the toilet with toilet paper. 'You'll have to call the plumber in the morning, love,' he said.

Harry got up, slavering on his fingers, and wiped his hands on the back of Sarah's hair.

'Oh, Mum! They've made my hair smell and I'm going to have to wash it now.'

'Get ready for bed whilst you're up there,' said Mrs Plantington.

Harry and Winston sniggered to themselves. They never got in trouble for anything. It was because they were so clever at acting daft, they thought.

The twins became more and more of a handful as they got older.
Eventually, when they were seventeen, a social worker suggested they should be placed in a supported living scheme as they were now older and it was only natural they should fly the nest, so to speak. Mother, although she loved the twins, wearily agreed. They were getting harder and harder to cope with as they got older. Neither of them would, or could, do anything useful round the house, in fact they did very little apart from causing mischief. Winston had taken to stuffing huge amounts of toilet roll down the toilet when he visited the lavatory. Dora thought it had been an achievement teaching the twins to use the toilet by themselves but she had to have the plumber out three times in one week. They always made a mess at the dinner table. In fact, they were always making a mess. They never spoiled the books she bought them but they where always ripping newspapers and magazines up. Particularly Sarah's *Jackie* and pony magazines — she was always in tears because they'd ripped it up before she got a chance to read it. Then her husband Ted got angry because they'd ripped the paper up and he wanted the television page. *He* was glad. He was glad they where going into care because now, perhaps, he could get his wife back at last. As far as he was concerned, it was about time she started to see sense; she was looking haggard these days she always used to take care of herself.

They would be sat there making mosaics on the floor out of the pieces of one of John's books or Sarah's pony magazine. The phone directory would get the same treatment if they didn't keep it in a locked cupboard. They were always breaking John and Sarah's toys. Harry had poured a bottle of shampoo over John's record collection. If they didn't like the clothes Mum had bought for them, they ripped them to shreds. Once, when grandma was baby sitting, they wound wool round the dining chair legs — unravelling her knitting. Poor John had got the blame for it.

John and Sarah were glad also that the twins were going to live somewhere else. The twins never seemed to get in trouble for anything. If they did anything half as naughty as the twins, they would get their pocket money stopped and be confined to their room for a week. However, the twins didn't get pocket money and they never went out with their friends, so there was nothing Dora could do but look at them with a sense of utter bewilderment. The twins didn't care about friends or money. All they cared about was each other and this silly game they were playing. It wasn't that they wanted their family to hate them. They loved their family but they craved even more. They loved being centre stage all the time and the world as they knew it revolving around them. Sometimes, they felt like the universe would not exist any more if anything happened to one or both of them. They took all of Mother's time. Sarah and John never seemed to get to spend any time with Mother as she was always too busy running about after the twins.

If they were not out with friends, John and Sarah were helping the stable hands mucking out, grooming and riding the horses. They both loved horses but it would have been nice to go away for the weekend like their friends did with their parents. To Blackpool, or something. Then they could go on the rides on the pleasure beach. Sarah would have loved just to have a day out clothes shopping with Mum, but she always had to go with her friends or Grandma or Auntie Joyce. Dad was always too busy with the stables to take them anywhere, particularly because Mum was so busy with the twins that she couldn't help as much.

It's not that John and Sarah hated the twins. They loathed them. They were their brothers but they were glad they were going to live somewhere else. Now, perhaps, they could get some much-craved for attention off their parents and they could leave things lying about without them getting ripped or broken. The twins were always taking their stuff to pieces if anything was left out. The twins had dismantled Sarah's little pink transistor radio that she had left on the couch. The twins' moving away was the best thing as far as John and Sarah were concerned. Dad agreed. He loved his boys of course, they where his image, but his wife wasn't the woman she used to be. She used to be so immaculately turned out and so composed. Now she always looked tired and haggard like she'd just dragged herself out of bed, and her nerves were completely shot. He felt it high time she gave over caring for the twins to the professionals and gave herself a break. He wanted his wife back, plus he could do with her helping out in the stables again like she used to. She'd had to give the R.S.P.C.A. animal hospital up as well as the twins got older and more of a handful, and he knew she wasn't happy at having to give up her hobby. She'd be able to start caring for sick woodland creatures again, using her talents, get back to her old self. He might even get her back to dancing to *Top of the Pops* on the radio like they always used to on Sunday evenings in the old 'pre-twins' days.

Dora herself had to admit that seventeen years was enough. She felt at screaming point most days and it wasn't as if they were sending them off to hospital. The social worker had suggested a nice little supported housing scheme. They would have their own house with staff coming in to support them. Even Dora had to agree it was time she handed over the reigns to someone else. Most children left home as they got older and they were going to live in a house — not, as she had dreaded for them, a hospital ward.

The only people not happy about the situation were the twins. They didn't fancy leaving home to be looked after by strangers. They began to wish they'd never started this stupid game; acting daft in front of everybody. They began to wish they'd acted normal like Sarah and John and helped out with the housework and with the horses instead of acting daft all the time. They were being thrown out of the family home and it was their entire fault. Still, they could hardly voice their opinion about it. Not after all these years keeping quiet. They could hardly come clean now after seventeen years and start acting sensible all of a sudden. What would people think? So, it came to pass that the twins went to live at Calder Fields Place, supported by Buttercups and Daisy Fields residential services for people with learning difficulties.

Chapter Three: Buttercups and Daisy Fields

Iris looked professional in her smart red skirt suit. Her dark red hair, neat and tailored, brought out the glint in her brown eyes that shone through the round, small-framed glasses that perched on the end of her nose. She sat cross-legged and leaning back on her chair, her black stiletto hanging lazily off her sheer stockinged toes, and filing her long red nails. Her matching red handbag sat on the desk in between the phone and the in and out trays. In the corner was a Yucca plant; it had grown to the ceiling then started winding along the roof towards the window, craving light. The phone rang. 'Hello,' she answered in a husky voice, 'Buttercups and Daisy Fields residential services for people with learning difficulties.' She pressed the phone receiver between her chin and her shoulder and continued filling her nails.

'Is Mick there?' asked the man on the other end of the phone, a sense of urgency in his voice.

'I'm afraid Michael is out at the moment. Can I help you?' said Iris, for once telling the truth about her boss's in/out status. She pictured him in her mind — his strong lean shoulders, his brown spiky hair. His deep brown eyes she could sink into. She had fancied him since she first set eyes on him. Pity he didn't feel the same way about her.

'Look, I started with really bad toothache last night,' said the man whose name was Nigel, a support worker in one of the houses. 'I've made an appointment at the dentist for this afternoon but Joan hasn't shown up yet. It's two-thirty and my appointment's at three o'clock. Joan was supposed to be here at two. Maybe she's not coming in but I need someone to cover. Tell Michael he needs to come and take over from me. I need my tooth fixing,' Nigel spoke agitatedly.

'I'm sorry, Mr Fenchurch didn't say what time he would be back,' said Iris apologetically. Nigel wasn't one to bother Mr Fenchurch unnecessarily.

'Well bleep him. This is an emergency!'

Nigel slammed the phone down, angry at the fact that Mr Fenchurch never seemed to be around when he was needed. He put his hand to his jaw and groaned, rubbing his neatly trimmed beard at the side of his face. Nigel really was in pain.

He sat down on the beige leatherette chair and glanced at the fish tank. A big black carp looked back at him with bulging eyes, making kisses with its mouth. At least the goldfish loved him, he thought to himself. Where was Joan? It was only her third shift; you'd think she'd be on time the first week at least.

The twins were now thirty years old; they sat on the couch side by side both wearing jeans, jumpers with triangle patterns and training shoes. They were brawny and handsome with Adonis-like blonde hair and blue eyes. They would have looked good in a gladiator movie. Nigel could imagine them racing horses with a carriage with spiked wheels. The two of them sat intently, staring at there fingers whilst wiggling them about. The doorbell rang. Nigel looked gratefully towards the door and then went to answer it. A lady wearing a skirt suit, stockings, high heels, makeup and perfect hair brushed past him and straight into the living room. She had a big holdall over her shoulder as well as a handbag. This was Joan — the newly appointed care worker to replace Jan who had left to go with her husband to live on a barge boat. The twins where glad Jan had left. It's not that she wasn't nice but she just treated them both like babies.

‘Sorry I’m late Nigel,’ Joan said panting. ‘My mum’s been rushed into hospital, so I’d nowhere to leave the baby. Luckily, her next-door neighbour was in so I left it there. I said to her, “What am I going to do? I can’t have her! I’ve got to go to work!” Anyway…’

‘Yes, well. Sorry, I’ve no time for hand over,’ interrupted Nigel. ‘I have to rush. The lads are fine. Bye.’ Nigel brushed past her and leapt down the driveway into his leaf green Volkswagen beetle. He glanced back at her through the rear view mirror and raised a hand in a half-hearted wave before speeding away.

Joan waved back and then disappeared upstairs to put her overnight bag into the sleep-in room. She found a magazine out on the dressing table and tutted as she tidied it away into a drawer. She came downstairs and started adjusting the brown floral curtains in the front window. Then she did the same thing with the dining room curtains. She came back in the front room and adjusted the ornaments on the mantle shelf, turning them and moving them a few millimetres. She then went round with her finger checking for dust. She tested the doorframes and skirting boards, tutting and wiping her finger on a tissue out of her handbag. Then she went into the kitchen. The two men stopped looking at their fingers. Winston picked up the TV remote control off the table, switched on the football and then put the remote on the couch at his side. The twins liked football. Joan came back into the front room. Both men started to rock backwards and forwards as they looked intently at each other’s wiggling fingers. They where discussing Joan. They didn’t like her very much. They hated living here. They wished they were still at the farmhouse with their family. Still, they loved winding the staff up and being the centre of attention as usual.

'Who turned the TV on? Has someone come in?' said Joan wide-eyed, unbelieving that the two men would be capable of such a simple task. She walked into the hall and looked up the stairs. 'Hello! Hello!' She looked back into living room and saw the TV remote control on the settee. She picked it up and waved it at the two of them.

'Don't touch! You'll break it!' she said, feeling daft that she was talking to two idiots who obviously didn't understand a word she had said. She turned the TV off and put the remote on a high shelf, not thinking that the men were taller than she was and could therefore easily reach it. She went back in the kitchen. The smell of cheep bleach began to waft into the front room with the sound of cleaning up noises.

'I was watching that,' signalled Winston.

'Yes, I want to watch the match as well,' signalled Harry.

'Have I to turn it back on?' signalled Winston.

'No, it looks too suspicious,' signalled Harry.

She returned with a tray, carrying two plastic beakers of pop and a plate of biscuits. She put a biscuit in each of the men's hands then watched as they crammed them into their mouths, spewing crumbs everywhere. She handed them a beaker of pop each, which they drank, spilling half of it down themselves. She tutted. This was like looking after two big babies — they spilled things and made a mess everywhere. She put the beakers back on the tray and disappeared back into the kitchen. The boys could hear the sound of washing up.

Harry and Winston started sniggering quietly. It was their way of winding new staff up; making a mess.

Joan walked back through the front room and into the hallway.

Winston whispered to his brother, 'She's gone to get the vacuum out.'

Harry whispered back, 'Have I to lie on the floor?'

'Yes! Yes!' sniggered Winston. He was holding in the laughter so much he had to wipe a snot bubble away with his sleeve.

Harry got up and lay down on the floor, legs up and crossed above him and wiggling his fingers in front of his face. Joan came back in with the Hoover and saw Harry on the floor. 'Oh no!' she said, despairingly. 'How am I going to vacuum now?'

'Is this so funny?' signed Winston.

'Yes. I have the best ideas sometimes,' signed Harry. 'This is really winding her up.'

She ran over and grabbed hold of the man's hands, trying to pull him up. Joan was getting fed up of this. Even though she had no training and no experience, she had spent one half of a shift with another member of staff before being thrown in at the deep end. She didn't know quite what to do with two idiots who couldn't speak and couldn't do anything, other than dress them, feed them, and stick them on the couch. She just wished they would stay put.

'Eeeeeeeee. Eeeeeeeeeeeeee,' screeched Harry.

Winston started to rock with his hand over his mouth. Joan went to the back of Harry and tried to push him up with his shoulders.

'Uuuurrgggghh, Uuuuurrrgggghhh,' said Harry in mock annoyance. He was enjoying this. So was

Winston, although he was a bit peeved that he hadn't thought of it first.

The phone rang and Joan picked it up.

'Hello! Yes there is an emergency. How did you know?' said Joan, amazed. 'Nigel rang? Oh, never mind,' she said, realizing they were at crossed wires somehow, but still wanting to take advantage of the emergency bleeper. 'Yes, I could do with you coming round. Thank you!'

Joan put the phone down and went into the kitchen. If in doubt, clean! She took all the contents out of the kitchen cupboard, put on rubber gloves and started to scrub the insides.

Winston whispered to his brother, 'She doesn't talk much does she?'

'No, she doesn't does she?' replied Harry

The doorbell rang. The two men stopped talking and started to examine the palms of their hands and wriggling their fingers again. Joan came through to answer the door.

'This must be Michael,' signed Harry.

'Yes, come for the emergency,' signed Winston. They both made the signal that they where laughing inside.

'So what's the emergency?' said Michael, stepping over the doorway like it was a railway sleeper. He was, as always, immaculately turned out. Today, he wore a pink shirt under a slate grey suit with a grey tie and black leather shoes. His hair was gelled into short but perfectly formed spikes.

'I can't get Harry up off the floor and I need to vacuum the crumbs off the carpet,' said a now red-faced Joan.

'Oh, well since I'm here, how about a nice cup of

coffee?' asked Michael. He didn't really think it was a call out emergency, but never mind now — he was here so he may as well stay and have a drink.

'Of course!' said Joan, returning to the kitchen.

Michael extended a hand out to Harry. 'Come on now Harry, stand up. That's a good man.' Harry stood up and sat back on the couch. Joan returned with the coffee.

'He's up! How did you do that?' she said, 'Obviously you're stronger than me.'

It didn't occur to her that he would have just asked the man to stand up. As far as she was concerned, the men could understand nothing.

'So, how was your first week?' asked Michael.

'Hmm…' Joan wondered where to start.

'Are you coming to the team meeting on Friday?'

'Yes, definitely!' Joan said — she couldn't wait to get her two pennies' worth in.

'Have you thought of anything you would like to bring up?'

'Oh, where do I start?' began Joan. 'The kitchen cupboards are a disgrace. Neither Nigel nor Julie knows how to open the curtains properly, and someone left a magazine in the sleep-in room. Can you believe that? These are supposed to be the staff.' Joan got a tissue out of her bag and dabbed her nose. 'The house is a disgrace.'

The two men started rocking and making uuurrgggghhhhhh noises. It was their way of registering their disapproval at Joan calling the other staff. They liked Julie and Nigel. Nigel was a pleasant enough chap, calm, collected and not easily excitable. But Julie? Julie was special. Julie was the only person who knew their secret. She had overheard them reading to each other from a magazine in the garden. They acted daft at first when she confronted them but she had persevered until eventually they started talking to her. Julie had tried to tell the other staff but they thought she was taking the Mickey or something. They started to treat Julie like she had gone mad until in the end she kept quite about them; an involuntary conspirator in the twins' deception. They were relieved nobody believed her. Sometimes, they wished they could stop this silly game of theirs. However, they would feel stupid coming clean after all these years. They had no choice but to carry on with it for the rest of their lives. Or so they thought.

'Oh dear!' said Mick looking at the men. 'Is there something wrong with the boys? They're making an awful fuss.'

'I don't think so!' said Joan, wondering what on earth Michael was talking about. They were always making funny noises.

'How dare she call Nigel and Julie,' signed Harry.

'I know, she's not all that,' signed Winston.

'I can't stand the way she keeps faffing about with the curtains and moving the ornaments about as if two millimetres matters.'

'I know, she's too fussy by half if you ask me,' signed Winston, and he made another uurrgghh noise to indicate that he didn't like her.

Mick looked at Winston, trying to work out what the matter was. 'Why don't I put the TV on for them? That might quieten them down.' Mick looked around for the TV remote and saw it on the shelf. He got up and retrieved it and turned the TV on. He was sure the men would get bored half the time.

'And I've checked the tops of the doorframes,'

continued Joan. 'They're filthy! The skirting boards obviously haven't been touched in years. It will take me weeks to sort this mess out, and why should I do it all? If everyone just did a little bit of cleaning every day, we might get somewhere.'

'Hmm…' said Mick totally disinterested — he had heard all this before. Michael was aware that not all the staff where perfect at cleaning but they had other talents. He certainly wasn't concerned whether the tops of the doorframes were shiny or not.

Mick's mobile rang on cue. Iris was an excellent judge of how long his house calls should last. He looked gratefully at his phone as he thumbed the key to answer.

'Hello Iris, what can I do for you?' Michael pictured Iris in his mind; her neat, perfectly coffered red hair, her red lipstick lips, her long lacquered red nails. He fancied her like crazy. So many times he had been tempted to make a move on her but he was scared she might slap him in the face and leave. She was a good secretary; he didn't know what he would do without her. Worse, she could sue him for sexual harassment. 'An *emergency* you say. Okay, on my way.'

He smiled at Joan. 'I'm terribly sorry but there appears to be an *emergency* in one of the other houses. I'll see you at nine in the morning for your first supervision.'

Michael didn't know what he would do without Iris. She always anticipated his needs. He hated listening to staff drone on and on about housework. There were more important things in life, he'd always thought. He left quickly, flicking the switch for his automated car door lock as he left the building, and didn't bother to wave.

'Humph.' Joan went back into the kitchen,

disgruntled that her moaning session had been cut short. This was worse than being left all day with the baby with no one to talk to and two big sodden lumps to look after. She'd only applied for this job thinking that she'd be working with other normal people and have some adult company and conversation. It would be an excuse to leave the baby with relatives. She hadn't realized she'd be left on her own with two big babies and loads of housework to do. She came back in the lounge briefly and searched in her bag for her bottle of perfume. She found it and sprayed her pulse points on her wrists and neck before returning the perfume to her bag and returning into the kitchen.

The twins watched the racing on the television.

'And it's Twice a Night, Twice a Night is the lead coming up to the fourth fence,' said the television commentator. 'Oh dear, and Twice a Night has fallen. What a tragedy. That looks nasty! Twice a Night was set to win but he's fallen at the fourth fence. The jockey has been thrown clear. He's standing up. The jockey's fine and the vet's running onto the racecourse. What a turn up of events.'

On the racecourse, a lady in her late fifties with a blue rinse perm and a pleasantly wrinkled face and piercing blue eyes, went running out to the injured horse. Three men — the jockey, the vet and the owner — were stood round the horse. The vet looked up and shook his head. The old lady said something to the men and they started shaking their heads. The lady started to wave her hands in the air, obviously hysterical, and the owner started making 'calm down' gestures with his hands and then turned away, scratching his head. He threw his hands in the air then looked at the lady with a puzzled expression on his face. The lady smiled at him and got out her mobile phone as it started to rain. She was ringing the R.S.P.C.A. to see whether, if she bought the horse, they could send out the air ambulance.

The twins watching didn't notice it was their mother on the TV. They were too busy signing to each other. She didn't usually go to the races but something had prompted her to go this afternoon. It was the anniversary of when her now dead husband had first proposed after bringing her to this very racecourse. She didn't really approve of racing horses; it upset her when horses fell and had to be put down. But her late husband loved racing and it seemed a fitting place to come on this special day. Now she was making such a fuss over this one fallen horse. The owner just wanted the horse put to sleep now its usefulness was over but that wasn't going to happen. Not if Dora had anything to do with it. She got her chequebook out of her pink gold-trimmed handbag and wrote him a cheque. The owner looked at the cheque and shrugged his shoulders and sighed. He looked at Mrs Plantington; a sad pleading in her eyes that were welling with tears. He nodded and put the cheque in his pocket and walked off briskly.

'I like Julie,' whispered Harry, thinking aloud.

'And Nigel. That Joan was calling them,' noted Winston.

'I don't like Joan,' whispered Harry.

'I don't like Joan either,' whispered Winston.

On the television, the commentator was astounded. 'Well, I've never seen anything like it in the history of racing.' A vet was giving Twice a Night a painkilling injection and an R.S.P.C.A air ambulance was waiting, hovering in the air to hook Twice a Night up.

'Someone appears to have called an air ambulance for Twice a Night,' said the commentator. 'I believe the horse has broken his leg. One would have thought the vet would have had the horse put down, but this is most extraordinary. Never in the history of horse racing have I seen anything quite like this. It looks like the horse is going to be air ambulanced away.'

The twins still didn't notice that it was their mother waving directions to the pilot in the helicopter as the rain started to reach torrential proportions. It never occurred to them that their mother would be at a race meeting. Both of them thought at the same time that the old lady resembled their mother but they knew she hadn't been to a racecourse since Dad died. They remembered her saying to John at Father's funeral after too much whisky that she was never going with him to another race meeting now that her husband had died. Too many horses got injured or died for her liking. She had asked John not to go anymore but he had just looked at her and said how he liked a little gamble, just like his Dad.

'What time is it?' asked Harry.

'It's six o'clock!' said Winston, looking at the clock.

'Are we not having any tea?' Harry was puzzled as they had usually eaten by now.

'I'm hungry,' Winston said, rubbing his growling stomach. 'Should I make something?'

'Don't be daft!' said Harry. 'Do you want Joan to know you can make something to eat?'

'No. I'm really hungry, though. I bet she's forgotten about us.' Winston turned the channel over to the news.

'We could have some fun with Joan tonight,' said Harry.

The two men started laughing and rubbing their hands together.

Joan, upstairs and oblivious to the twins' plotting, climbed onto a bedroom chair to clean the windows. Joan hated any sort of mess or disorder. She was a bit of a perfectionist as far as neat and tidiness was concerned. She continued cleaning till late, almost forgetting about the twins and the fact they needed feeding and putting to bed. She couldn't have gone to sleep herself, not with the house a mess. Suddenly, she decided to look at her watch.

'Oh my God is that the time?' she said to herself. 'I've not made any tea yet.' She rushed back downstairs, looked in the freezer but couldn't find anything simple to make. 'Oh these will do,' she said, finding some crumpets in the breadbin. She put them in the toaster.

'Is this all we are having?' Harry and Winston both signed as two plates with four crumpets each were presented in front of them. They ate them, their stomachs growling.

'I can't believe this is all we're having,' signed Harry.

'Uurggh, Uurrgh,' said Winston.

'Right.' whispered Harry when Joan had gone back into the kitchen to wash up. 'Tonight's payback time.'

Winston grinned and nodded. They started signing madly about what their devious little plot to wind Joan up would be.

Chapter Four: Saving Twice a Night

The rain had stopped from its torrential proportions and the warm sun had made an entrance from behind the clouds. The smell of hay mingled with the smell of wild roses and honeysuckle that grew in the field Dora had left for the wildlife. The foxgloves and gymslips moved graciously in the breeze, giving up their sweet scent into the air. Bees buzzed and butterflies fluttered around, hovering and pollinating the vast array of different coloured flowers. The field was a riot of colour. A kestrel swooped down in a spiral and caught a vole that was hiding in the grass, and then flew up to a tree branch to eat its meal. It pulled at the flesh with its beak, holding the vole in one claw and the other holding the branch.

By the field, at the other side of the hedgerow, a horse stood regal with a young child on its back. Its tail softly swished back and forth to move the flies away. Stood in front holding the reigns was Sarah, who had grown into a beautiful woman. She wore her blonde hair bundled into a bun at the back of her head and had strong, piercing blue eyes that resembled her mother's. She was wearing her red riding jacket and cream jodhpurs with black riding boots. The gentle wind blew wisps of hair around her face as she led the horse with a child on its back onto the riding enclosure.

'That's it! Back straight! Well done!' she said.

The child smiled and pursed her lips in concentration sitting high in the seat; she flicked her riding crop as the horse trotted round in a circle.

John walked past the rows of horses in the paddock. He always walked about with purpose, as if he was on his way to an important business meeting. He resembled the twins but looked slightly older and not as stocky. He had inherited his mother's slender frame. He had the same blonde hair and blue eyes as the rest of the family. He always looked immaculately turned out, even when in casual dress. Today, he wore stonewash jeans and a blue t-shirt with training shoes. He was handsome with his floppy, slightly wavy blonde hair that framed his face and chiselled features. He had been in the office sorting out the stables' finances when the commotion outside had prompted him to investigate. The horses whinnied and reared up, stamping their hooves on the concrete in animated protest at the noise made by the helicopter blades whirring overhead. John looked up as he walked along. He could see a helicopter making for the paddocks and what appeared to be a horse in a sling suspended underneath. 'What the Hell?!' he exclaimed.

A jeep pulled up and a very wet Dora got out. Her summer dress clung to her wet body and her hair fell limp and dripping round her face. Her mascara had run, giving the impression of two black eyes. She started walking towards the approaching helicopter.

'Mother, is this you're doing?' shouted John, his voice barely audible over the noise of the helicopter blades.

Two young boy stable hands ran forward. John watched in confusion and disbelief as they ran towards the old lady.

'Get the horse trolley,' shouted Dora, now high on adrenalin.

A stable hand ran back to the stables and fetched a huge wheel along a collapsible trolley that Dora used for sick animals.

'Has the spare stable at the end got clean hay in it?' she asked the stable boy, grabbing the trolley.

'Yes, Mrs Plantington,' replied the stable hand.

The helicopter hovered in the air, suspended like a giant bird as the boys and Dora guided the horse onto the trolley and then unhooked the cable. The air ambulance then flew back up into the air and landed back in the field. One of the R.S.P.C.A. men climbed out of the helicopter and walked towards Dora.

'The boys will show you where to put him,' said Dora as he approached. The R.S.P.C.A man followed the boys, helping to push the trolley.

'Mother, what on Earth are you up too?' shouted John. He was red faced and his blonde hair was untidy and windblown by the helicopter.

'You've talked about buying a racehorse,' said Dora in a matter-of-fact way.

'WHAT?! A RACEHORSE?! THE THING'S PRACTICALLY DEAD!' he shouted in disbelief. His mother really took the biscuit sometimes. He wondered if she was going mad in her old age. Of course, he'd always thought she was a bit mad with her obsession with sick animals. He wondered whether he should call a psychiatrist out and get her sectioned. If she thought the stables' money was paying for this little project of hers, she had another thing coming.

'Of course he's nearly dead, you stupid boy. How else could I get a racehorse for two-thousand pounds?' Dora said, following the trolley with her eyes. The horse was certainly in a worse condition than she originally thought; she had no intention of letting it out of her sight at least until morning.

'You paid for it?! Two thousand pounds? Good God Woman!' shrieked John. 'You'll be lucky if it's still alive in the morning. Mother, what on earth were you thinking?' John despaired of his mother and her habit of bringing hurt and injured animals home. She'd never gone as far as a horse before, though. It was usually birds and the odd hedgehog.

'How do you think I got him for two-thousand pounds, you stupid man? If the owner thought for a minute he was going to live until morning he never would have sold him me for that price. He thought I was barmy as well. Anyway, it's a good horse. If it hadn't fallen at that fence it would have won!'

His mother astounded him with her logic. 'What do you mean, "if it hadn't fallen?" Obviously it *did* fall. What's the use of owning a dead racehorse! You *stupid* women! He saw you coming, didn't he, eh? He wouldn't get two-thousand pounds at the knackers' yard would he?' John threw his hands in the air. 'Even if it does live, it's no use to anybody. It won't be able to run properly again, and nobody would be able to ride it.'

Dora was scared her son was going to burst a blood vessel. 'Sorry. Haven't time to argue with you,' she said, running after the horse. She knew her son was right; her only thought had been that she felt she could make the horse well again. She was sure he would pull through with the right sort of care and attention. Her caring nature had taken over. She hadn't given a thought to what she was going to do with the horse once it was better. The owner hadn't been too keen to sell him, despite the fact that it was going to be put down, but Dora was a woman of much persuasion — she had appealed to him and broken him down to the human side of his nature, even though she knew that most racehorse owners only cared about the money. She had given him a fair price, she thought, although the owner wanted more. Eventually, she had managed to reason with him and he had given in.

Rodney, the R.S.P.C.A vet, helped pull the horse off the trolley with the sling and the help of several stable hands. He was an unimposing man of five feet two inches, but he looked smart in his R.S.P.C.A uniform. His brown, almost black hair had been coffered into a double cowlick at the front. His dark brown eyes were very revealing and showed compassion for the horse he was treating. He had a mole on his left cheek and huge dimples that cratered when he smiled. He was the sort of man that women wanted to take home and mother.

The horse was sweaty and in obvious distress, but thanks to the injection it had been given it wasn't in any pain. Rodney gave the horse another shot of morphine just to make sure. When he was sure the horse was comfortable, he walked back through the paddock to where the helicopter was waiting to take off.

'Thanks George. I'll stay here for a while. I'll see you at the station tomorrow,' Rodney said, leaning on the helicopter with an outstretched arm.

'Okay Rod!' George replied. Rodney stepped back as the whirring started, and the helicopter rose into the air, ruffling Rodney's hair and starting another round of whinnying and hoof stamping in the paddock. He watched with a hand over his eyes as the helicopter slowly disappeared into the distance.

John came running across the field to him, distressed and breathless.

'Rod, why did you let her do this?' he said panting, leaning over with his hands on his knees. 'You always pamper to her. You could have tried talking some sense into her or something.' He stood up straight and put his hands on his hips, still panting.

'You know your mum John!' he stated by way of explanation and scratching his nose and looking at the floor. His face flushed slightly.

'Oh come on!' said John. He was shouting again and waving his arm about pointing. 'You must have had to pull some strings to get them to send a bloody helicopter out for God's sake.'

'No, not really,' insisted Rodney, looking John briefly in the eyes before looking down at his shoes. He shuffled his feet in the dirt. 'Your mum has done a lot of work for the R.S.P.C.A. and held lots of money-raising events. It was her efforts that bought us that helicopter. Anyway, your mum has helped a lot of sick animals in the past. She has a way with them. As you know John, she's something of a legend with the R.S.P.C.A. and if she thinks there's a chance he'll pull through, then we think there is too. Anyway, the helicopter is there to save animals in distress.' Rod stood up straight, hands in pockets, and puffed his chest out. 'Look John, you know how much I think of your mother. I'll never forget how kind she was to me when I was a child. I would never have passed my degree in veterinary medicine if it wasn't for your mum inspiring and supporting me.'

'Oh, you're as bad as she is. I'm going back to the house!' said John, storming off. Rod had been John's childhood friend; at least he started off as his friend but had ended up more of his mother's friend. Colluding with her, bringing her little birds with broken wings he had found in the forest and helping her to splint them. Helping her to mix her little poultices and potions, tending to the sick animals, or else she was helping Rod with his homework. He never remembered spending an awful lot of time with Rod himself, although he was always at their house when he was little. What was it with Mum? She always had time for waifs and strays and sick animals, but never for him. First, it was the animal hospital, then the twins; she was always running about after his twin brothers because they had learning difficulties, and then it was the animals again. Perhaps he thought if he broke his leg or something he might get some attention from her. He was too independent — that was his trouble. He didn't need her; he wasn't needy like the sick animals, or the twins, or Rod when he was little. Now it was a stupid dying racehorse that was going to be taking up all her time. What on Earth had possessed her to buy a dying racehorse? What use was a racehorse with a broken leg? Even if by some miracle she did manage to nurse it back to health, they wouldn't even be able to use it at as a riding school horse. Stupid, stupid women, he thought.

John reached the house and unlocked the heavy oak door that led into the kitchen. He walked through into the lounge and opened a big globe that hid a decanter of whiskey and six lead crystal glasses. He poured himself a glass and sat on the Chesterfield wing-backed chair that had always been his father's before he passed away. Father had been gone two years now. John had been devastated when he was killed. It had been a riding accident. Dad had been breaking in a new filly in the farmer's field when a gun had gone off. The filly had bolted. Dad was an expert rider but hadn't been able to hang on as the horse darted out of control. He had fallen off the horse backwards, landing on his head, breaking his neck. They'd sent a search party out looking for him when the horse eventually returned to the stables on its own. John had found him. He had tried to resuscitate him and called 999 on his mobile phone. They had sent an air ambulance out, but it was too late. He was already dead. It wasn't just losing father that had affected him. The accident had reminded him of his own mortality, how fragile life really was. God gives us life but life can be taken away so easily, he had thought. So easy to have a fatal accident or catch some life-threatening strain of flu. Then there's cancer, leukaemia and all the rest of it. John had felt frightened to get on a horse for a while. Dad had been an expert rider. If it could happen to him…well, it could happen to anyone. He'd had to force himself to get back in the saddle. Still, he was nervous when riding; looking round for anything that could possibly cause a horse to bolt. He was particularly nervous around traffic when riding along roadsides. Riding was definitely a chore these days, rather than the pleasure it used to be.

John sipped his whisky and started to mellow. He was the head of the household now and in charge of the family business. He couldn't believe Mother had paid two thousand pounds for a dying racehorse. It was a good job he had control of the stables' finances. He had a vision of what it would be like if Mum was in control. No riding school. Just stables full of sick and dying animals. Ah well, he thought, draining the last dreg of Glenmorangie from his glass. He loved Mum, despite her eccentricities. He decided he would just have to let her get on with it. After all, it was her own money she bought the horse with. If she wanted to spend all of her hard-earned cash saving dying animals, that was her prerogative he supposed. Although he hoped she was going to pay the costs of feeding it and everything. Why should the stable finances pay for her little project? He thought about how she hardly spent a red cent of her money on anything else. She didn't smoke, she didn't drink much or gamble like him. She only bought new clothes when her old ones got holes in them. She must be loaded, he thought to himself, she's got half the stables' profits. He only got 25%, yet he was doing okay financially; he had investments. He thought briefly about leaving a ball lying on the stairs, and then quickly shook it out of his head. He poured himself another glass of Glenmorangie and put *Madame Butterfly* in the CD player. He was feeling pleasantly relaxed now and all of a sudden he didn't care very much about anything anymore. He finished off the whisky and then drifted off to sleep in the chair.

Chapter Five Revenge on Joan

Night-time fell over Calder Fields Place, the full moon shone spreading a silvery glint on the rooftops. The street lamps shone for the night creatures and a stray dog ate chips from a discarded newspaper. The snuffling sound it made echo around the otherwise silent estate. A cat started calling out, making a sound like a crying baby. A pair of bats fluttered about, catching insects to take back to their forbidden nest in somebody's rafters. The twins' rafters. They had a little family of four baby bats.

The lamplight shone through the thin summer curtains into the twins' bedroom. They had two single beds with *Thomas the Tank Engine* duvet covers that Jan had bought them, with bedside cabinets separating them; they also had a wardrobe each. There were shelves also, with cuddly toys and videos on them. The twins were both in bed, fast asleep. Harry suddenly woke up and sat up in bed rubbing his eyes. He got up and tiptoed across the landing and put his ear against the other bedroom door. He could hear Joan softly snoring. He smiled to himself; time to put his plans into action. He tiptoed back into the bedroom and whispered, 'Winston, Winston, wake up.' He shook Winston to wake up.

'What is it?' asked Winston, bleary eyed and forgetting for a moment the devious plans they had made earlier.

'Shush!' said Harry. He made the sign that meant he was going to do something naughty. Winston smiled as he threw back the bedclothes; he knew what his brother had in mind. This was "get back at Joan time". Harry signalled with his hand for Winston to follow him. They both tiptoed downstairs. Their bare feet made no sound on the carpet; both of them prayed the floorboards wouldn't squeak.

They stood looking around the front room. They had to cause a big mess somehow. Joan didn't like mess. Yes, Joan would definitely be unimpressed — if not hysterical — when she woke up in the morning, thought Winston to himself, especially, after all the time she had spent cleaning the day before.

'What exactly are we going to do?' whispered Winston

'I know!' whispered Harry. 'Help me pick the T.V up; let's put it on the floor.'

Winston and Harry picked up the television and put it carefully — screen side down — on the living room floor.

'Careful! Don't break it! Tee, hee,' said Winston. He was finding it very difficult to laugh quietly.

The twins stood looking at the television, wondering what to do next. Winston went into the kitchen and started rummaging in the cupboards. He came out of the kitchen with a bag of flour in his hand. 'Look what I've found,' he said as he started emptying the contents of the bag around the floor.

Harry put his hands over his mouth to muffle his sniggers and then got a chair and pulled it towards the window. 'I know what will wind her up. Watch this.' He unhooked several of the curtain hooks so the curtains sagged untidily. Both of them were having difficulties holding back the sniggers.

'Shush, she'll hear us,' warned Winston as he went round the room adjusting all the pictures so they were really crooked. Harry went into the kitchen and reappeared with some cocoa powder. He sprinkled it round the living room. Winston smeared jam on his face.

Harry followed suit, giggling gleefully. Harry moved all the ornaments about on the mantle shelf. He'd noticed how she'd moved them around earlier, like two millimetres made all the difference. This would really upset her. They took the papers out of the magazine rack and sat on the floor, ripping them into tiny pieces and then scattering them around the living room floor.

'This will show her. Calling Nigel and Julie,' said Winston.

'Look what I've found,' said Harry. 'Chocolate sauce. We'll smear this all over ourselves as soon as we hear her get up.'

They both sniggered. If this didn't get steam blowing out of her ears, nothing would.

Harry and Winston sat on the couch. They needed to stay awake until morning. Winston decided he would tell Harry a story; something they often did when nobody was listening. He whispered as quietly as he could into Harry's ear.

'Once upon a time,' started Winston, 'there were a pair of twins that liked looking up to the stars. One night, they where walking in a park when they spotted a shooting star. The star got bigger and bigger until they realised it was a spaceship. The spaceship landed and a big alien got out. It looked like a cross between a lizard and a human. The alien looked hungry, so one of the twins — Harry — got his peanut butter sandwiches out of his satchel and gave one to the alien. The alien ate the sandwich, although he said being a lizard he preferred eating insects. He asked the pair if they would like to go for a ride in his spaceship. So they said "yes". They got into the spacecraft and it flew off into the sky and into outer space. The twins saw all the constellations close up; Aries, The Big Bear, Capricorn, and they saw nebulae and black holes. They flew through the rings of Saturn. They flew past Mars and Venus. Then the alien took them visiting other planets and they met all sorts of different types of aliens and each planet they visited had different types of food to try; different types of wine to sip; different types of music to listen to. The twins made lots of new friends until eventually the alien said it was time to go home and he took them back and dropped them off in the park. He said if they wanted to go off in a spaceship again, they should just stand in a field and one of their new friends would pick them up'

'That would be nice,' said Harry, 'meeting an alien from outer space and going off in a space ship with him. Do you think aliens really exist?'

They had had this conversation many times before. When they were young, Mum used to have barbecues on balmy summer evenings and they would get to stay up late. Mum used to put a rug out for them on the grass. They would lie on their backs once the sun went down and look up at the stars. Sometimes, they would see flashes of light streak across the black satin night sky. They wouldn't discuss it at the time, but later when everybody was asleep they would discuss whether they were meteorites, comets, or alien space ships.

'Well,' said Winston, leaning his head on his hand and his elbow on his knee like the thinker. 'I think it's arrogant of us to presume that in this whole great vastness of a universe we are the only intelligent life forms. So yes, I think aliens exist. Whether they have technology to fly through space and whether they have visited us or not are different matters.'

'That's right,' said Harry. 'The nearest star to us is more than four light years away, and one light year is 9.46 million, million kilometres. So they would have to have a very, very, fast spaceship indeed.'

'Still, who would have thought two hundred years ago that we could be in Spain in two hours? Or that we could visit the moon?'

'That's right,' said Harry. 'Who knows what technology alien life forms have? They could have cloaking devices like on *Star Trek* so we can't see them.' He paused and they both looked at each other. 'Here,' he said. 'I've got a story. Once upon a time, there were two twins whose mother owned stables. They grew up and helped to look after the horses and their mother was really proud of them.'

'Oh don't,' said Winston.

'What are we doing Winston?' asked Harry. 'What are we doing with our lives? Living here, being looked after by strangers. Why did we start all this? Don't you wish we'd just grown ourselves up normal like our John and Sarah?'

'It's too late for regrets now,' said Winston. 'People expect it of us; they expect us to act daft. We can't suddenly start acting normal now and ask Mum if we can help out in the stables. Mum would have a heart attack.'

'Still, I'm going to enjoy seeing the look on Joan's face when she comes down. Where does she get off calling Joan and Nigel like that?' asked Harry. He laughed quietly — his shoulders shaking

'I know. I can't stand the woman myself,' said Winston grinning. 'Look at this mess, she'll go mad when she sees it.'

'I've got one.' whispered Harry. 'The twins went out in a field and waved and the alien came down, and it dropped them off in Las Vegas in America. The twins had a fiver each but they gambled in the casinos until they both had one million dollars. Then they bumped into Courtney Cox and Jennifer Anniston. They asked them out and they said “yes”. They took them out to a posh restaurant where they had champagne, caviar, and lobster. Then the twins dropped engagement rings in the girls' champagne glasses. Both of them accepted. They went back to the hotel room and Harry kissed Jennifer and Winston kissed Courtney and before you knew it they were all naked, indulging in a steamy sex session...'

'Oh stop,' said Winston. 'I'm getting a severe hard on.'

'… and they all got married in a double ceremony that night in Las Vegas,' continued Harry. 'Then they went back to a hotel with a Jacuzzi. They all got in the Jacuzzi naked and drank champagne, and then they all got into a big four-poster bed and had sex again. Hot, steamy, passionate sex.'

'Oh stop,' said Winston. Both of the twins were still virgins but they had learnt about sex from the television and videos the male staff brought in. It was a constant source of midnight discussions that they'd never have a girlfriend. Never get married. Never feel the pleasures of the flesh. They were doomed to die lonely old virgins.

'Then they bought a big house between them,' said Harry, 'with a swimming pool and they both had two kids each; two boys and two girls.'

'That would be nice,' said Winston. 'Nothing like that's ever going to happen for us though is it? We're never going to get married and have kids. We're never going to have girlfriends or a job or any of the things normal people have. We're both stuck on this scheme until we're old and grey.'

'We can dream though, can't we?' said Harry. 'I

wish we'd never started playing this game. We could be at home now with Mum and John and Sarah, helping them to run the stables. We could both have girlfriends.'

'I know, but it's too late to change anything now,' said Winston. 'We can't just start acting normal all of a sudden. We have to act how people expect.'

'I'm hungry,' said Harry. 'Imagine, crumpets for tea; it wouldn't have fed a mouse. Do you want a sandwich?'

'Yes, okay.'

Harry went into the kitchen to make some salmon paste sandwiches. They ate them, washed them down with a glass of milk each, Winston washed up, and then he came and sat down again on the couch.

'It would be nice to have girlfriends,' said Winston. He knew it was their own fault that they had ended up in this predicament. It had been fun when they were small — acting daft all the time — but now he really wished they had acted normal. They could have been at home now helping to run the stables. Taking young ladies out.

'Yes twins. Twin girls,' said Harry, rubbing his foot that was curled up on the couch.

'We'll get out of here one day,' said Winston.

'How?' asked Harry, picking his toenails and throwing them on the carpet

'I don't know yet.'

Both of the twins felt there was a better life waiting for them, somehow, somewhere. It was just how to achieve it.

Chapter Six Herbs and Potions

Oil lamps lit the stables, casting shadows over the walls and hay. Dora worked in the lamplight; Rodney squatted, watching her endeavours intently. Dora had been feeding the horse cold herbal teas through a large dropper. Now, she carefully sewed the horse's splinted leg with suture. It looked like there was a lot of blood but Dora thought the horse would soon make that up. He hadn't cut any major arteries and they had been pressurising the wound to minimise blood loss. Mrs Plantington had trained as a vet but had given veterinary medicine up when she had married Mr Plantington to help look after the stables.

"Do you think he'll make it?" asked Rodney. Personally, his professional opinion was the horse wouldn't make it through the night, but Mrs Plantington was a bit of a miracle worker with her unorthodox potions and faith healing.

'We can only do our best,' she replied, 'and pray.'

'Remember when I used to bring you injured animals from the forest?' said Rod. 'You used to fix them up, take care of them, and then we'd go and release them into the wild.'

Rodney remembered squirrels, birds and hedgehogs lined up in little cages; all the injured animals that local people had found and brought to her. She used to let Rodney help making poultices and potions out of herbs from her garden. Rodney was sure this was why he had wanted to be a vet. His training had taught him orthodox methods of treating sick animals but he did sometimes use some of Dora's herbal teas on animals recovering from surgery. Rodney had his own practice in the village but worked for the R.S.P.C.A part-time. He got paid expenses and a small fee for his time and trouble.

He was very grateful to the Plantingtons; they had always treated him like one of their own. When they first met, John had brought him home from school to have dinner at their house. He had been a scruffy little urchin with holes in his knees. Rodney's parents had died in a house fire when he was little. Leaving him at grandma's house, they had gone out for a drink. They had come home drunk from a night out and decided to make chips. Then they had both fallen asleep. They had left the chip pan on which had set alight, burning the house down with them inside it. Rodney remembered his father had taken the batteries out of the smoke alarm as it was always going off because of the toaster. Grandma had been too old and ill to look after him full-time so he had ended up in the children's home. He had been very angry and very bitter. He was angry with God, angry with his parents for dying on him, angry with Grandma for not being able to look after him, angry with the workers at the children's home for not being able to pay him enough attention. He was angry with anybody who had a better life than he did. Meeting John, or rather meeting Mrs Plantington, had changed his life. He was constantly round at their house, helping "Mrs P" (as he called her) with the sick animals. It was then he decided he wanted to be a vet. Mrs P had helped him with his biology and chemistry homework and supplied him with the references he needed for university and later to become a vet. He looked up to Dora. She was his role model. He had never met anyone so kind and warm-hearted who helped people so much without asking for anything in return. She had a special gift with healing as well. She was a much better vet than he could ever hope to be. Not that he was a bad vet — he was very good indeed. It was just that Mrs P had some kind of God-given gift for healing animals and making them better. Dora was a miracle worker.

'Of course I remember,' said Dora. 'You and John were best pals then,' she smiled. 'Pass me the oil.'

Rod passed her a jar of red-coloured oil and Dora poured it onto a cloth and put it over the horse's wound.

'How are the twins?' Rod asked.

'Oh, you know them, they never change,' she replied. 'They're still with Daisy Fields. I was never really happy with them leaving the family home but I suppose everybody was right. I needed a rest. I had them at home for seventeen years you know and, well, they could be a bit of a handful. I've always said there's more to them boys than meets the eye. Sometimes, I could swear when I was in the kitchen I could hear them having a conversation. I kept saying that those boys were having us all on. They were all there with their cough drops. They were just amusing themselves at our expense. My husband said I was going barmy with caring for them all those years. I kept expecting to wake up one morning and they'd be two normal young men that would be able to help in the stables. I still hold that thought now you know. One day, they will wake up and all their problems will disappear and, well, they'll do something to make me proud.'

Rod nodded as he mixed plaster of Paris mixture in a bucket. Dora applied the poultice and held it in place with a bandage. She loved caring for sick animals. She was sure he would pull through with a little tender, loving care.

Rod soaked some bandages in the plaster of Paris

mixture, and then between them they applied the bandages to the horse's leg.

'I've never plastered a horse's leg before,' said Rodney

'There's a first time for everything,' said Dora.

When they had finished, Dora poured some cold herb water into the horse's mouth. 'We've got to keep him hydrated,' she explained. Rod nodded. 'I'm going to stay here all night and keep an eye on him,' said Dora, covering the horse with a blanket. 'I expect you have to go Rod?'

'I could do with getting some sleep. I've got a bitch to spay first thing in the morning. Then I'm removing a tumour from a gerbil. Can you manage without me now?'

'Yes, thanks for helping me with the plaster. I couldn't have managed without you.'

'You're welcome,' said Rod, and he took Dora in his arms and kissed her passionately. Dora felt her toes curl. The first time Rodney had come on to her, she was taken aback; he was old enough to be her son. However, she had always loved the boy as far back as she could remember and she was sure her departed husband wouldn't mind her having a new love now he had passed over. It wasn't as if Rod was a blood-relative and, anyway, men had affairs with younger women all the time.

Rodney put his hand up her jumper

'Not now Rod,' she said breathlessly. 'I have to look after the horse.'

Rod smiled and stepped back. As always with dear Mrs P, the animals came first. He worshipped the ground she walked on. He couldn't believe he was having an affair with her. He was shy with other women but it all felt so natural with her. The first time he kissed her she had slapped him. Then she had looked at him all confused and kissed him again. They had ended up making love in the hay on the floor of the barn. He often wondered what John and Sarah would have to say if they found out he was having it away with their mother. He bet they wouldn't be too impressed. Still, they wouldn't find out, he thought to himself. Their affair was a big secret.

Rod phoned a taxi from his mobile phone. 'I'll call by tomorrow and see how he's doing,' he said.

The taxi came and Rod left. Dora went back to the cottage to shower, change and fetch herself a flask of coffee, a sleeping bag, a radio and some pillows. She got inside the bag, although she'd no intention of going to sleep. She poured herself a coffee and drank. Dora could see the stars through the top half of the stable door, which was open. It was a clear night and the stars twinkled. She wondered what was out there, up there. Were there other inhabited planets out there in space? Were there spacemen flying past and watching us in our little houses? They could be watching us like we belonged to some sort of soap opera. Dora sipped the strong, sweet, warm liquid. She wished Ted were here. She felt a little bit fearful camping out here at night on her own; she had a gas lamp and a torch but still it was dark. The silence was eerie, the horses were very quite tonight and all she could hear was the wind and the sound of crickets. The odd owl hooted. She got up and fed the horse some more herbal tea through a dropper. She stroked his back. Then she sat back down inside her sleeping bag and poured herself some more coffee to stay awake.

She intended giving the horse fluids every hour,

so she had to stay awake. Plus, she wanted to be there in case he took a turn for the worse. She turned the radio onto the classical station. Tchychovski's *Nutcracker Suite* was playing. She was reminded of a record she had bought for Sarah when she was little; Charlie Chester's *Featherbed Fairy Tales*. The Sugarplum Fairy tales, told with the classical music playing in the background. She remembered back to when there was just John. Before the twins and Sarah were born. Life was a lot simpler then. She had been so proud of her first baby, dressed in a powder-blue knitted suit, hat and gloves, she had paraded him round the village in his cot. She spent all her spare time knitting things for him. The stable hands and villagers had cooed over him and picked him up and fussed over him. He had been three years old when the twins were born and she had terrible problems with him wanting attention all the time. He hadn't understood that he couldn't demand the same attention of her now that two new babies had come along. Everything was old-hat when the twins were born. She certainly didn't have time for knitting anymore; besides, you could buy clothes just as cheap readymade in the shops. Then, when Sarah came along two years after that, John had pulled terrible tantrums because Mum couldn't attend to him immediately. The twins demanded her attention, so did John, and then she had a beautiful little baby girl to look after. Looking back now, she didn't know how she had coped. The twins alone were enough of a handful to deal with. She felt John was still a little resentful of anything that took up her time. Like the animals; she was sure that's why John had caused so much fuss about the racehorse. She felt he would like her all to himself if he got a chance. The twins, well, they where just the twins. They had a way of demanding attention whether you wanted to give it to them or not. Sarah had always been used to having to share her mother's attentions. She had always been a good little child that didn't mind amusing herself with her dolls and things. Dora felt sure she would have been grateful if they could have spent more time together, but she had never complained. She'd always played by herself, then, as she got older, helped with the household chores without complaining. She'd helped out in the stables as well. Helping the stable hands to muck out and groom the horses. She'd always been very industrious. It went without saying that she would work in the stables when she was older. John as well; he always complained about having to wash up or put the bins out but he was always eager to help out in the stables. John was running the stables well since the death of her late husband. He was a bit of a whizz at balancing the books and always coming up with new advertising campaigns to get more customers. Profits had doubled since John took over. Inspired by the twins, he'd even invested in special hoists so they could take disabled riders — and they had quite a lot of disabled riders on their books. They also did a horse trek on a Sunday when people could come in on a one-off and go trekking down the country lanes. He really was business-minded. The twins, well, Dora had a dream that one day they'd recover from whatever it was that was wrong with them and make something of themselves. But it was just a dream.

She wondered what her children would say if they found out about her and Rodney. It didn't bear thinking about. She just hoped they would never get caught. They'd just have to be careful, she thought to herself. After all, she may be their mother but she was still a woman with needs. So what that Rodney was so much younger than her? He made her feel like she was still attractive, despite her aging years. She wondered what she'd do if Rodney ever found a woman more his own age. It was bound to happen — he was an attractive young man. She'd just have to cope with it, she supposed.

Chapter Seven   Left in the Lurch

Back at Calder Fields Place, the alarm clock began to ring out its morning siren. Joan's arm reached out of the duvet to turn it off. Wearily, she sat up and rubbed her eyes. She walked into the en-suite shower room and turned the shower on to warm up before going back into the bedroom to take her night clothes off. Yawning, she walked back into the shower room. She washed herself and her hair under the shower, softly humming. She had a good, firm body that she achieved through aerobics and going to the gym once a week. She came out of the shower and dried herself and shaved her legs and her armpits with an electric razor. Then, she put on a pink towelling dressing gown. She began to blow dry her hair, cursing because it wasn't going how she wanted it. She kept wetting her hair and applying more gel until, finally, she got it perfect. She then applied lots of hairspray, coughing with the fumes. Then she carefully applied her makeup; face cream, foundation, eye powder, eye liner, mascara, blusher, lip liner and lipstick, which she blotted and reapplied twice before applying lip lock. She thought the first think she would do when she went downstairs was to ring pest control — she'd heard some weird animal sounds in the middle of the night. Perhaps they had rats or something. No wonder with the state of the house. She got dressed into her skirt suit, but not before spraying herself all over with body spay. She looked at herself in the mirror and pouted, adjusting a section of her fringe. Then she took the hairspray bottle and gave her hair one final blast. She picked up the body spray again and sprayed it down her blouse and up her skirt. She examined herself in the mirror again, all over, adjusting her clothes, before going out onto the corridor.

She opened the door to the men's room and looked puzzled as to why they were not there. She went downstairs and opened the living room door to be confronted with the mess. Winston was sprawled on the settee and Harry was stood facing her with his pyjama bottoms round his ankles. He had chocolate sauce smeared down his legs.

Joan's face contorted as she let out a blood-curdling scream beholding the unholy mess in front of her eyes. The neighbours' bedroom lights went on and the curtains began to flicker. The sun was coming up a yellow/orange crescent over the rooftops as Joan made her exit out of the front door and off down the street, never to return.

'I don't get paid enough for this,' she muttered under her breath as she hurried off home.

'That worked well,' said Harry, sitting down next to Winston on the sofa. They both looked at each other and then started to roar with laughter, clutching their stomachs and rolling around on the couch.

Nine o'clock sharp and Michael's baby-blue Rover Estate pulled into the driveway. 'That's funny, what's the door doing open?' he muttered to himself, alarm bells going off in his head. He set the alarm on his car with his remote and made towards the door.

'Joan!' he shouted, going inside. 'JOAN?'

He opened the living room door. The two men where both asleep on the couch. He searched the house, shouting for Joan. He went back into the living room and sat on a chair, scratching his head. It appears, he thought to himself, that Joan has left us in the lurch. He went into the kitchen to make himself a coffee and some toast. He came back into the living room, turned on the television and started to watch the breakfast show whilst he decided what to do. He wondered what had happened to Joan. Maybe she'd just gone to the shop, he thought hopefully. He decided he'd give her half an hour before he did anything. His mobile rang; he took it out of his pocket and held it to his ear.

Iris's silky smooth voice purred down the phone at him. He imagined her standing virtually naked in a pair of red stilettos; he didn't know what she looked like naked but his imagination made a good guess. The very sounds of her voice made him feel all quivery and excited. He felt a stirring in his trousers and desperately tried to replace the image with Roy Hattersley before he got himself out of control.

'Hello Iris,' he said slightly breathlessly. 'No need for the emergency routine; Joan appears to have gone. Yes, gone! *Yes*, left the boys alone,' he said, standing up off the chair. 'I really don't know, but the boys certainly aren't happy. It looks like they've woken up hungry looking for something to eat. God knows how long they've been on their own. Listen, ring the agency and try to cover Joan's shifts. You better ring her at home and try to find out what's happened. I suppose it's possible she's gone to the shop or something. It's looking like she's left us though. I don't believe this. We're two staff down as it is. I wish people wouldn't keep leaving us.'

Michael stepped forward and heard a crunch. He looked down to see he had trodden on a raw egg. 'Oh no! Look, I'm going to ring Julie. See if I can get her to come in.' He hung up his mobile and went over to the landline phone, walking raw egg into the carpet as he moved his feet. He picked up the receiver and dialled. It started to ring. 'Come on, come on, pick up the phone,' he said, muttering under his breath. The phone made a clicking noise.

'Hello, this is Julie,' said a shrill, high-pitched voice. 'I'm sorry I can't come to the phone at the moment so please leave your message after the bleep.'

'Hello Julie, Mick here! I'm in a bit of a situation. I wondered if you might be able to come in early. Please ring me as soon as you get this message. Thanks.'

He put the phone down and looked around at the mess. What was he going to do if Julie couldn't come in? He had staff shortages all over the scheme. What if there was an emergency in one of the other houses? His mobile rang and he answered it 'Hello Iris,' he said, feeling all quivery again but hoping for some good news.

'Hello Michael,' said Iris. 'Bad news I'm afraid. Nigel rang to say he's been to the dentist and he has an impacted wisdom tooth. They are going to operate and he's going to be off for the rest of the week.'

'Please tell me you're joking!' Michael implored. 'Impacted wisdom tooth? Off for the rest of the week, *at least?'* Michael sighed. 'Oh well, you'll have to ring the agency and try and cover his shifts as well.'

'And I've rung Joan. She said something about not getting paid enough and she'd rather be at home with the baby. Anyway, she's definitely not coming back.'

'I wish she'd work her notice. She's not going to work her notice is she?' Michael was feeling desperate. He only had Julie left. He should have five staff members working at the twins' house and now he was reduced to one. He just hoped they'd be able to cover with agency staff.

'I'm afraid not,' said Iris, feeling sorry for Mr Fenchurch. It was hard work getting enough staff to cover the scheme properly. He always had to fill in for people when really he should be in the office doing the paperwork.

He put the phone down and looked around at the mess. ‘Oh dear, where do I start?’ Tiding up and cleaning was definitely not Michael’s strong point. Anyway, he was the boss. Why should he have to clean up? He didn’t do years of training and work his way up the ladder to be a cleaner. Michael went back into the kitchen and made a big plate of toast and some cups of tea. He put them on the table in front of the two men waking them up. The men woke up and ate and drank. He sat back down watching Breakfast T.V.

. It was now eleven-thirty. The men had gone back to sleep on the settee. The house was still a mess. Michael was sat on the chair reading a paper and drinking his tea. He had wiped the raw egg off the bottom of his shoe with some kitchen roll but it was still all over the carpet. The phone rang. He picked it up.

‘Hello, what’s the problem Michael?’

‘Julie! Thank God! Could you possibly come in early?’

‘How early?’ asked Julie.

‘As soon as possible please.’

‘I can possibly get there in half an hour,’ said Julie, looking at her watch.

‘That would be great!’ said Michael, sighing with relief.

‘I take it this is overtime?’

‘Oh, I’m afraid I can’t pay overtime — that won’t be possible. You can take it back as time owing…’

‘Forget it Michael. I’ve already got thirty hours time owing that I can never seem to take back. Bye.’

‘Wait….. Julie! Wait! Okay, on this occasion I

will make an exception and pay you overtime rate. Just get here as soon as you can. *Please.*' Michael sighed. He hadn't really wanted to pay overtime rate — he was over budget this year as it was. Julie had him over a barrel though; she knew he couldn't get any one else in at such short notice.

Michael was upstairs on the toilet reading the paper when the doorbell rang. He stood up and sorted himself out and then ran downstairs and opened the door. Julie, a plump lady with wavy unkempt hair, wearing jeans, jumper and trainers with no make up and glasses entered the room.

'Hello Mick' she said, opening the living room door.

'Oh my God, look at this mess! What the hell's going on?" she exclaimed.

Michael followed her sheepishly, putting his head round the door.

'*What?* I don't believe it! *Five minutes* I've been upstairs. I just went to the toilet. *Five minutes*! I really don't believe it. Look at this mess! *Five minutes*! The boys have made this mess in *five* minutes. I really don't believe it.'

Julie looked at him incredulously. 'Why have the twins still got their pyjamas on?' she asked.

'Look, I'm really sorry Julie; I really appreciate you coming in early. Unfortunately, I have to rush. There's an *emergency* in one of the other houses.'

Michael left hurriedly, pointing his remote at his Rover to turn off the alarm, jumping into the driver's seat and speeding off. Julie looked around the room at the mess, which now included a plate and glasses on the coffee table, surrounded by spilt tea and toast crumbs.

'Winston! Harry! What the hell is going on?' screeched Julie.

The two men woke up suddenly and jumped to their feet. 'Sorry Julie,' they chorused in unison.

Julie looked at the men and held up the palms of her hands towards the ceiling. 'Well?' She waited for an answer but none was forthcoming. 'Okay, I'm not going to ask again. I'm going to make a start on lunch. When I return to this room, I expect it to be returned to its former condition.'

Julie went into the kitchen. She didn't know what was going on but she certainly wasn't cleaning the mess up. The two men started busying themselves. Harry got the vacuum out and Winston picked up the television and started to put the pictures straight and everything right again. Winston went into the kitchen to get a cloth to wipe the raw egg off the carpet. Julie started banging the cupboard doors in the kitchen

'What the...' she shouted. 'Who's moved everything? Where has all the packet mixes gone? They were in this cupboard. They've disappeared. Harry, Winston have you moved them?'

'No Julie,' they replied in unison. 'It'll be that Joan.'

Julie frantically opened and closed the cupboard doors in the kitchen, inspecting the contents. Eventually, she found a Tupperware box and took it down. 'Oh, here they are. Someone's put them away tidy.'

She took some chicken pieces out of the fridge and put them in a casserole dish, and then she started to peel some carrots and cut some mushrooms up.

After about twenty minutes had passed, Harry came into the kitchen with the plates and glasses and put them in the sink. 'We've finished Julie!'

Julie looked round the door and into the living room. Everything had been restored to normal. She smiled pleasantly.

'Right then, go and get showered and dressed.'

The two men rushed upstairs into the bedroom. They got undressed and took turns in the shower, washing off the jam and chocolate sauce. They picked out exactly the same clothes from their respective wardrobes, without even looking at each other. They put on orange shirts, black trousers and black shoes. Then they slicked their hair back with hair gel. When they arrived back downstairs, the table was set. They sat down at the table and Julie came in with lunch.

'This is very nice Julie,' said Harry. 'Chicken chasseur isn't it?'

'Yes, à la packet mix.'

'Still, it's very nice!'

They both tucked in hungrily.

'We didn't get any dinner last night,' moaned Winston as he tucked into his lunch.

'Why not?' asked Julie.

'That Joan didn't make us any.'

'We had crumpets at half past ten with low fat spread on,' remarked Harry, picking the chicken leg bone up to suck on it.

'Is that why you made the mess?'

'And she said you and Nigel can't open the curtains.'

'What you on about? I always open the curtains.'

'Still, she's gone now,' said Winston and Harry in unison. It hadn't been their intention to drive her away, just to wind her up a bit. They weren't unduly upset that she had gone though; neither of them had liked Joan. She was far too fussy.

'You two are terrible! I'd tell on you if I thought they'd believe me.' Julie was dying to share her secret of the twins with someone else but when she'd tried to tell Michael he'd almost accused her of attention seeking, and suggested she see the scheme's counsellor. She'd decided it was better just to keep quiet and carry on doing her job. She preferred working on her own with the twins; they were much better behaved than when other staff members were on duty with her.

The phone rang and Julie answered it.

'Hello, this is the Plantington residence. Can I help you?'

'Hello, this is Mrs Plantington,' said the voice at the other end of the phone. 'I wondered if I might call round to see my special boys this evening.'

'Of course you can,' replied Julie. 'They're both here.'

'About six p.m. Will that be okay?'

'Six will be perfect. I'll see you then.'

Julie put the phone down. 'That was your Mum. She's coming round later. So whose turn is it to wash up?' she asked the boys.

'Harry's,' said Winston. 'I did it last night.'

Harry got up dutifully and went into the kitchen and began washing up. 'I haven't seen Mum since last week,' he said. 'I wonder what she's been up to.'

'Probably still saving sick animals,' said Winston. 'I wonder how John and Sarah are doing.' Winston envied John and Sarah still living in the family home with Mum. He missed the stone cottage with the leather Chesterfield in the lounge and pine table in the kitchen. He missed having lessons with Mum. He missed the smell of her famous country soup, wafting through the house from the kitchen. He missed John and Sarah coming home smelling of hay and horses. He missed home. It wasn't the same here. Okay, it was nice winding the staff up and having fun in that respect but he missed the cottage and his family. Harry felt exactly the same way.

'John's the head of the stables now with Dad dying,' Winston said. 'I wonder if he's managing okay. I wonder if they're still in profit.' Winston was still upset that he and Harry hadn't inherited a share of the stables when their Dad had died.

'I don't know,' said Harry, rinsing a plate under the tap. 'You realise if anything happened to John we'd be the heads of the stables.'

'You two, head of the stables?' laughed Julie. 'I think not. I think it would go to Sarah and skip over your heads, so to speak.'

'Why's that?' asked Winston. 'What's wrong with us? Why couldn't we run the stables? We'd be good at it,' he said, leaning forwards and clasping his hands in front of himself.

'Yes, we're good at maths and things. I'm sure we could manage the finances,' said Harry, shouting from in the kitchen.

'Yes, but nobody knows that, do they, with you two acting daft all the time?' said Julie. 'Everybody thinks you've got severe learning difficulties. Who's going to let you two take charge of the stables? Get real!'

'Oh yes,' said Harry. 'I never thought of that.' Harry finished putting the dishes away and put the kettle on.

'No, you two don't think, do you? Of course, you could come clean and tell everybody you've been playing them up and tell them how sorry you are.'

'Too late for that,' said Winston.

'Yep, too late,' said Harry.

Harry came in the front room with two cups of tea.

'Did you not make me one?' asked Julie.

'Oh, I'm sorry — I forgot,' said Harry, sitting down. He picked up the television remote control and put the news on.

'I'll make my own then,' said Julie, getting up and going into the kitchen.

Chapter Eight Young and in Love

Dora was in the stable with Twice a Night. She put her mobile phone away and looked at the horse, which was still lying on the floor. She was overcome with compassion for the poor thing. Ever since being a small child, she had loved animals and she hated to see them being cruelly treated, or in pain. She crouched down beside the horse and felt up the plastered leg. Well, the plaster of Paris had set well, she noted. She got up and went over to a table in the corner of the stable and took a bowl of liquid over to the horse and squeezed it into its mouth using a cloth. She stroked the horse's head. 'Come on boy! I know you're strong — you can make it.'

The horse neighed and struggled, trying to lift its head off the ground.

'Come on babe, get to your feet. Come on,' encouraged Dora.

She stroked the horse's head again. The horse neighed and raised its head, and then started to struggle to its feet. Its left foot was splayed in front of it in plaster of Paris. Finally, the horse made it to its feet. Dora threw her arms round the horse's neck. 'Good boy! Well done! You did it!'

She led the horse to the trough to drink and stroked its back. Dora had loved being a vet; she wondered what would have happened if she hadn't met Ted and given it all up for him. She would probably have had her own practice by now. She'd be spaying cats and pampering people's poodles. Not that she was resentful; she had loved Ted with all of her heart and she enjoyed helping out with the horses at the stables. A tear welled up in her eye as she remembered how close she and Ted had been.

She missed him so much. She remembered when they were courting and he had taken her to the races. She had been so young then, dressed in a pink floral dress with matching hat, jacket and pink sandals. Ted had put two pounds on a horse, which was a lot of money in those days. The horse had lost but Ted wasn't a sore loser. He still took her out for a meal that evening — some posh Italian restaurant — Rigiatallio's she thought the name was. That was when he proposed. He got on bended knee right there in the middle of the restaurant. She played with her diamond engagement ring, twiddling it on her finger. He was no cheapskate, Ted Plantington. It was a beautiful stone. She had accepted of course. Ted was kind and loving and a hell of a good catch, what with him owning the stables. She had quite a good job herself; she was a junior in a vet's practice in the village. That's how she met Ted. She used to come out to his horses when they were sick. He'd asked her if she'd like to go riding one weekend and she accepted. One balmy summer's day they'd spent walking the horses through the farmer's fields. The next week he'd invited her on a picnic. They'd sat in the field that Dora now left for wildlife, near to the river. He'd brought sausage rolls, smoked salmon, roast beef sandwiches and a full box of chardonnay. They got pleasantly pissed and that's when he had kissed her for the first time. Sparks had flown and Dora thought her heart would nearly bust. They had left the picnic and gone back up to Ted's office where they had made love on the desk, in amongst the riding hats crops and saddles. Explosions had gone off. Luckily, the stable hands had gone home, otherwise they would have heard her moaning in ecstasy. Ted had tickled her thighs with a riding whip as he thrust his manhood inside of her and she had climaxed again and again. Dora filled up with emotion as she remembered the sweet first encounters with her darling late husband. Her voice let out a stifled croak and she clutched her chest as her heart started to race. She felt a pain shoot up her left arm and she leant against the stable wall, gasping for breath. Presently, the pain subsided and she stood upright again and began to groom Twice a Night. She felt a brief twang of guilt at her affair with Rodney. She was sure if her husband was looking down on her he'd understand she was a woman with needs.

Dora had been saving up to start a practice of her own but all that had fallen to the wayside after marring Ted. She had given up veterinary medicine to help him with the stables and look after the children.

She remembered how in the good old days — pre-children — they used to go riding together every Sunday. They would gallop, racing each other in the fields and then trotting up the lane to the Farmer's Arms. There was a field at the back where they could tether their horses whilst they went inside and had a meal. They would emerge a few hours later, slightly merry, and saunter back down the lane to the stables. Then, once the horses were safely stabled, they would sit in the kitchen listening to music on the radio and drinking whiskey. Sometimes they would get up and have a dance around the kitchen. Then they would go up to the bedroom and make love. Dora wiped a tear from her eye. Life was so unfair. Why had Ted been so cruelly taken away from her in the prime of his life? Dora had been looking forward to a happy retirement. She had envisaged at some point that Ted would hand over the reigns to John and they could go abroad for holidays. Dora had only ever been out of this country once. She went to Spain with some student friends when she had been at university. She had enjoyed experiencing a different culture. Ted always liked to be within a few hours' journey of the stables, just in case anybody needed him. She had imagined once they retired they could go on a cruise or somewhere exotic like Africa. She could just see herself on a safari in the khaki clothing taking photographs of lions and giraffes. She'd mentioned as much to Sarah and she'd suggested that the two of them go, but it wouldn't be the same without Ted. It had been her dream that that would be what they were going to do when they both retired. It wouldn't seem right to go without him.

Dora put her arms around Twice a Night's neck and hugged the horse. He was, she thought, a testament to her healing skills. It was good to have a project to keep her mind off things. 'Well, I'll have to leave you to it now,' she said, not the least bit embarrassed at talking to a horse. 'The stable hand will be round to see you with food later on. I have to visit my other special boys tonight.'

Dora looked back fondly at Twice a Night, still drinking from the trough, as she left the stable.

Chapter Nine Motherly Love

Dora sat on the couch balancing a china teacup and saucer on her knee. Julie sat on a chair opposite with a mug of coffee. The twins knelt crouched on the floor, looking at some books.

'They've always enjoyed looking at those astronomy books I bought them,' commented Dora. 'They were always looking up at the stars when they were little.'

'Yes, they look at those books a lot,' said Julie.

'I always knew they were different, the twins. They didn't learn to speak like the other children, but I know they communicate with each other. They have a special bond that only twins have.' Dora watched the twins reading on the floor and smiled at them, her eyes full of love.

'I've noticed that,' said Julie, slightly bored with the conversation. Mrs Plantington said the same things every time she visited.

'Are they coming horse riding this Monday?' Dora asked. The twins still went horse riding every Monday — rain or shine — and they still loved it as much as ever.

'Yes, they'll be there as usual,' sighed Julie.

'They're very intelligent in their own way,' said Dora, putting her empty teacup and saucer down on the dark oak wood coffee table.

Harry got up and went running to his Mum, putting his arms round her neck. Mum smiled and hugged him back. Winston brought one of the books to his mother and pointed to a constellation.

'Yes, that's Libra; your star sign. You know don't you?' Dora winked at him and kissed him on the cheek.

Winston laughed and went to sit back down with the book.

'It's obvious they love you,' remarked Julie wearily. She tired of the twins' games and wished they would just act normal and sit on the couch and talk to their mum liked they talked to her.

'They may be different but they're my boys and I love them both! Oh, but they didn't half give me trouble when they were born. Twenty-five hours I was in labour. Harry came first then Winston half an hour after that. I nearly died when I found out I was having twins. Still, I wouldn't swap them for the world, despite their problems. I know I shouldn't say this but I always felt more for the twins than their brother and sister, despite, well you know, they being how they are. They both remind me so much of their dad. They have his hair, his eyes, his nose, his smile. I know it sounds daft but I keep thinking one day the twins will suddenly get better. Do something with their lives. Do something to make me proud. It's just a daft, doting mum's silly fantasy. They're both so handsome; it's a shame they're never going to get married.'

She looked at her watch. 'Anyway, I have to get back before it gets dark. Bye my darlings,' she said, smiling at the twins. She put her teacup down on the table, and then went over to the twins and kissed both of them on the cheek. Looking at them was like having Ted back in duplicate. She smiled and wiped a tear from her eye with the initialled handkerchief she kept in her pocket.

Julie saw Mrs Plantington to the door. 'Bye, Bye, Mrs Plantington. Take care,' she said waving her off.

'You too, Julie dear,' said Dora, climbing into her Land Rover.

Julie came back into front room and stood looking at the twins with her hands on her hips. 'Why do you not talk to your mum?' she asked. 'She's a lovely lady.'

'It's habit!' replied Harry.

'Yes! It's too late now!' agreed Winston. 'Too late to change it.'

'Too late to tell mum now' said Harry

'I don't know!' Julie exclaimed. 'I wish I wasn't the only person in the world who knows you two can speak. If only I hadn't forced the issue that day I heard you talking in the garden, I'd be in blissful ignorance like everyone else. Trouble is, every time I try to tell anyone they look at me as if I'm barking mad.'

Julie sighed and sat down and turned the television on. Both the twins got up off the floor and started watching the news on the television.

'And now the sports news,' said the commentator. 'At Aintree, Twice a Night was air winched off the track by an R.S.P.C.A. air helicopter after it had fallen and broken its leg. Mr Yarrow, the owner, was about to have the horse put down when a Mrs Plantington, who offered to buy the injured horse, approached him. Twice a Night's new owner was unavailable for comment this afternoon. Mr Yarrow said the lady was 'barmy' but most insistent that she wanted to buy the injured horse. He said Mrs Plantington was most persuasive. He felt he had got a good price for the horse considering the circumstances in that he doubted the horse had long to live. He said if the horse did live, she'd got herself a bargain, although its racing days are definitely over.

'Blimey,' said Harry. 'That's mum. She never said. Mum's bought a racehorse.'

It was a bright and warm summer's morning and

the light flooded in through the window. Birds could be heard twittering outside as they lined up on the telephone wire for a gossip. Harry busied himself vacuuming the carpet whilst Winston polished the ornaments on the mantle shelf. Their shirts where wet with the sticky heat. A fan droned away on the window ledge; it gave small comfort from the heat of the day. They were in the middle of a freak heat wave. When he had finished, Winston disappeared upstairs and came down again with a laundry basket full of clothes. Julie sat at the dining table with paperwork in front of her.

'Have you sorted that out into whites and dark colours?' asked Julie.

'Yes!' replied Winston as he disappeared into the kitchen.

'I have to fill your toilet sheet in. Winston have you had a B.O. today?'

'No!' replied Winston.

'Yes,' replied Harry. 'I had a massive one. I couldn't get it to flush.'

'Thank you Harry,' said Julie.

Winston took the empty laundry basket back upstairs, Harry put away the vacuum cleaner and both of them sat on the settee. The doorbell rang. Both men started twiddling their fingers in front of their faces and rocking backwards and forwards.

'Who's this now?' signed Harry.

'Don't know,' signed Winston in reply.

'Oh pack it in, please!' said Julie, exasperated. She didn't realise the twins were signing to each other. It was just them messing about as far as she knew.

Both men start grinning. Julie answered the door. A smart looking Asian man, dressed in a black suit, was standing outside.

'Hello,' he said. 'My name's Sunil, the agency sent me.'

'Come in Sunil,' said Julie, leading him into the front room where the twins were still acting daft on the couch, 'This is Harry and Winston.'

'Hello there!' said Sunil nervously.

Winston looked at him blankly, sucking his finger, then clapped his hands and laughed. Harry smiled and rubbed his hands together.

'So, can they speak at all?' Sunil stood with his hands in his trouser pockets, rocking on his heal.

'Oh, they do sometimes. When they're in the mood,' said Julie, glaring at the twins. 'Come on, I'll show you the paperwork.'

Julie led Sunil into the dining room. Money tins and various recording books and sheets where scattered over the table.

'I'm taking over from you again tomorrow, so don't worry too much if you don't get everything done,' said Julie. 'Michael's on call if you need him. His number is here in this telephone book. There's a toilet programme for the twins here. I think it's pretty self-explanatory. You just need to record when they open their bowels so we know if they need their laxatives or not. I don't think you'll need any money. If you do, take it out of the household budget tin and book it out in this book. The receipts go in this little envelope at the back. Hmm, I don't really know what I can tell you about the twins. Just do your best. Good luck.'

Julie patted Sunil on the shoulder then picked up her handbag and made towards the door.

'Oh, I was just wondering,' said Sunil. 'Do the boys like spicy food? Or should I make pie and chips for tea?'

'Oh, the twins love curry and spicy stuff,' replied Julie. 'Their mum used to make stuff like that all the time. I make them curry and they really enjoy it. Anyway, bye bye and good luck!'

She waved at Sunil as she left and walked off briskly down the path. Sunil went into the kitchen to see what he could make for tea. He found some cook from frozen lamb chunks in the freezer and there was, to his pleasure, a full and well-stocked spice rack. Mmm, Lamb Rogan Josh, he thought to himself. He fried the lamb with some onions and then set about adding his spices. He set a big pan of rice on the boil, simmering. When it was nearly ready, he started looking in the plate drawers. He found two special scoop plates. 'These must belong to the boys,' Sunil muttered to himself. 'I don't know! No one tells you anything.'

'That's a nice smell wafting from the kitchen.' signed Harry.

'Yes, better than crumpets,' signed Winston.

Sunil found two thick-handled spoons in the cutlery drawer. He presumed these must be for the twins as well. He went into the front room and shouted the twins to the table. Neither of them moved; they just sat staring blankly at him, sucking their fingers. Sunil went into the front room and led them one by one to the dining table. He sat them down and tucked napkins under their chins. He brought in the special scoop plates full of curry and put them in front of the boys. Then he brought in his own plate and sat down. He started to eat and then looked at the twins. Both of them were just sat staring at their plates but not touching it.

'Come on boys, I was told you like curry,' said Sunil. 'Come on, try it. It's nice! Harry. Here, put the spoon in your hand.'

He got up and put the spoon in Harry's hand. Harry looked at him and scooped up some of the curry with the spoon and put it into his mouth. He started to make a 'mmm… mmmmmm' sound.

'That's nice isn't it?' said Sunil, pleased that his culinary efforts were being appreciated.

Harry and Winston started picking up the curry with their hands and ramming it into their mouths. Sunil got up and ran round the table.

'No! No! Use your spoons!'

He put the spoon in Winston's hand and scooped up some curry, hand on hand. 'Like this!'

The twins were enjoying winding him up. There was nothing the two of them liked better than having some fun, particularly with new staff. They had nothing against Sunil, if anything he was too nice. So far, he didn't shout and always seemed to keep his calm. Harry and Winston wondered how far they could push him before he eventually cracked and lost his temper. Winston stole some food off Harry's plate using his hand; both of them were dying to laugh but they resisted the temptation.

'No Winston, eat your own,' said Sunil, exasperated.

Winston returned to his own plate but was still using his fingers. Harry picked up his plate and started pouring food in his mouth off his plate. Sunil surveyed the scene, hands on hips.

'Oh dear, what am I going to do?' Sunil paused to think. 'I know! I'm going to eat *my* dinner in the other room.' The twins were putting him off his meal and making him feel sick. Anyway, he thought it best if he just ignored them.

He picked up his plate and went into the front

room. He shouted back at them.
'At least you're eating it. You're not going hungry. You like my curry huh?'

Harry and Winston had to admire his cool; a lot of staff would be screaming and shouting at them by now. He was staying calm and collected; they had to give him brownie points for that. They decided they liked Sunil but that didn't mean they were going to stop winding him up.

Sunil finished his meal and took his plate into the kitchen. He came back into the dining room and surveyed the scene. There was curry and rice everywhere, all over the twins' — their faces, their hands, all over the table and all over the floor. Sunil sighed. He took the boys one by one up into the bathroom to wash their face and hands and brush their teeth. Then he sat them down on the couch in the lounge. He had tried to wipe the curry from their clothing but they were all stained with curry spices. He then set about cleaning the dining room, wiping the curry and rice off the table and hoovering up.

Winston and Harry started signing to each other as to how they could wind Sunil up.

'That's the last time I make you a special curry! Next time I come here, it's sausage and chips with green beans. Or something else that's easier to pick up. Oh, look at this. Bloody Hell. Look at this, there's rice everywhere,' he said, using the vacuum tool to suck the rice up off the seats where they had been sitting.

Sunil finished tiding up and made all three of them a nice cup of tea. Then he settled down on the chair and put the television on. Just in time for the match, he thought to himself. Man United were playing Liverpool. All three of them were watching intently. The twins were quiet and well-behaved; they liked watching football. It wasn't often they got to watch sport on the television. Julie always let them watch what they liked when she was on duty. Then again, she was the only person who knew what they liked. The match was just about to finish when Man United score a goal. All three jumped up and shouted.

'Yes!'

Sunil turned round to look at the men. 'You like Man United?' he asked, surprised at hearing them speak.

There was no response from the twins. He got up off his chair and went and stood in front of them and shouted. 'Yes!' hitting his fist in the air.

The twins copied him shouting 'Yes!' and hitting their fists in the air.

'Yes!' shouted Sunil as he waved both hands in the air.

'Yes!' shouted the twins as they waved their hands in the air.

'Hmm. interesting,' said Sunil. He couldn't understand why they suddenly shouted 'yes' when they had been so quiet and unresponsive all evening. He couldn't quite put his finger on it, but something about the twins didn't add up — didn't make sense. 'Anyway,' he said, 'come on. Time for your shower and get ready for bed. Come on Winston.'

He took Winston by the hand and led him upstairs. He opened the bathroom door then turned around to find Harry had followed. 'No! One at a time in the bathroom, please.' He took Harry across the landing to the bedroom. 'You wait in here please!' He went back to the bathroom and started to help Winston take his top off. He looked over his shoulder to see Harry was at the back of him again. 'No, wait in the bedroom.' He took him back into the bedroom and returned to the bathroom. He again started to help Winston get undressed. He sensed something and looked over his shoulder to find Harry was behind him again. He ushered him out, closing the door firmly behind him. 'Is there no lock on this door?' he asked frantically.

He started to help Winston again; Harry opened the door and came back into the bathroom. Sunil shoved the now naked Winston under the shower. Then he undressed Harry and put him in the shower cubicle as well. Then he stood on a stool to wash the rice and curry out of their hair. 'Oh, stuff procedure,' he muttered to himself. 'It doesn't matter. You're both men aren't you? You're both brothers aren't you?'

Harry and Winston wondered why he hadn't just asked them to go and get showered. It was a mistake a lot of staff made. They just assumed that they'd need help in the bathroom. Mum had always washed and dressed them as well. They were used to it. Julie was the only staff member that asked them to have a shower. All the other staff washed and dressed them. They wouldn't have gone to have a shower by themselves if he'd have asked. They would have just looked at him blankly, acting daft. Still he could have asked them first instead of just presuming they needed help. Sunil got them both dry and into their pyjamas, and tucked them both in bed. Then he took the clothes downstairs and put them in the washing machine. He had just sat down with a cup of tea when the twins came back down the stairs and sat on the couch. Sunil sighed and went into the kitchen to make them a milky drink. After about half an hour, he took the twins back upstairs to bed and got himself ready for bed. He set the alarm and snuggled under the covers in the sleep-in room. After about twenty minutes he drifted off to sleep. He had just started to sleep soundly when he was awoken suddenly with a jerk. He realised with a panic that he couldn't move his legs. Then he realised it was because the twins where sitting on them. The twins weren't tired yet. It was only early as far as they were concerned.

'Oh no,' said Sunil. He managed to wriggle his legs free and then took the twins back to their room, only to find they had pulled all of their bed sheets across the landing. 'Oh no, I'm going to have to make your beds again now.' Sunil made the beds and tucked the twins in, then went back to his own bed in the staff sleep-in room. He couldn't get back over to sleep again; he tossed and turned all night, finally falling asleep about five o'clock in the morning.

Chapter Ten Country Soup

The smell of hay and horse manure lingered in the cool evening air. Crickets had started to rasp their mating chorus. Rod and Dora stood in the horse's paddock, both of them wearing green Wellington boots and overalls. Rod was feeding some fresh grass out of a bucket to Twice a Night that stood balanced on three legs. One leg was splayed out slightly in front of him, still in plaster.

'I knew you could do it Mrs Plantington,' said Rod. He was lying; he would have put good money on the horse not lasting the night. 'You really are a miracle worker.' Rod didn't know how Mrs Plantington did it. He wouldn't even have attempted to try plastering a horse's broken leg. He would have put the poor thing down, like most vets.

'Healing is 50% know-how and 50% love, care and affection,' Dora said. 'You can teach people the mechanics of medicine…'

"But, at the end of the day, you need to believe and be able to will things to get better; healing is a gift. You taught me that Mrs P.' If anyone could cure someone just with pure willpower alone Mrs P could, thought Rod. In all his time as a vet, he'd never met anyone with such a talent for healing as Mrs Plantington. He was in awe of her. She was his inspiration.

'That's right! Nothing aids any being's recovery better than knowing that people care and want it to get better. I have to admit in this horse's case, if it does recover due to my loving care and attention I may ask it to repay me in a certain way.' Dora had no idea what she was going to do with the horse that day she ran out onto the racecourse. She just felt sorry for it. She felt certain she could nurse it back to health. She hadn't thought about the fact, as her son had so eloquently pointed out, that the horse would be unfit to ride again. However, a plan had formed in her head. She could stud him out. She'd been researching his form and he had a good track record. Okay, he'd be unable to take weight on his back but he could still father foals, she thought to herself. People would be willing to pay a good price for Twice a Night's genetic material. She knew it.

'Well it nearly got put down by lethal injection,' Rod pointed out. 'I'm sure if the horse can help its saviour in any way it wouldn't mind.' Rod couldn't think what Mrs Plantington's devious plan could be. As John had pointed out, the horse couldn't be ridden again. Rod was surprised the plaster had stayed put. He thought the horse's leg would break again as soon as it put weight on it, but the horse seemed to know not to put weight on it and was managing somehow to hobble along on three legs. Rod wouldn't have thought it possible.

Twice a Night made a whinnying sound.

'How long do you think we'll have to keep the plaster on for?' he asked.

'About six weeks I'd imagine,' said Dora, who had started to groom the horse's mane.

'Do you think it can manage on three legs until then?'

'I hope so. He's a strong horse; he's got a strong spirit.' Dora started to groom the horse's tail. 'Do you think I should put it in plaits?'

Rod laughed. 'You're putting him through a dressage competition already?'

'No, no, don't be daft. I just thought it might help him feel better if he looked smart. Yes, I will put it in plaits.'

Rod laughed again. He couldn't get over Mrs Plantington's enthusiasm and optimism. He stuck up for her of course, but secretly he'd felt John was right. It had been a crazy thing to do, rescue a racehorse with a broken leg. Yet, here it was standing up, eating grass and having its tail plaited. He had always been in awe of Mrs Plantington. He hadn't known of an animal die on her yet.

Dora finished plaiting the horse's tail then got a bottle of herb water and a dropper out of her bag and started to feed it to the horse. 'Rod, could you get some more fresh grass from the field? It needs fresh food to recover properly.'

'Yes madam,' said Rod. He picked up his bucket and headed out for the wildlife field. 'Fresh grass,' he muttered to himself. 'Must be fresh grass.' The sweet smell of grass and wild flowers wafted out on the breeze to meet him. The sound of buzzing bees and crickets rasping their legs filled his ears. He plucked the grass that grew between the wild flowers and put it into the bucket, and then when the bucket was full he headed back to the stable, swinging it at his side. He put some of the grass in his flat palm and fed it to the horse. It ate hungrily.

'Well,' said Dora. 'I don't think there's anything else to be done. Fancy a whiskey?'

'I'm driving,' said Rod.

'Just one,' said Mrs Plantington, temptingly.

'Well, okay,' said Rod, hanging the now empty bucket on a hook in the corner of the stable. He patted Twice a Night on the neck as he passed him to leave the stable.

They both walked back to the house and entered through the heavy oak door into the kitchen.

'Hmm…' said Rod, sniffing up. 'Something smells nice.'

'That's my country soup, would you like some?' She went over to the stove and put a light under the big pan that sat on it before going into the lounge to fetch two glasses of whiskey.

'Who could resist your country soup?' asked Rod, sitting himself at the pine kitchen table. Dora's country soup was legendary.

The kitchen was quite large with an old fashioned cooking range that the soup sat upon. There was a pine dresser that displayed fancy plates and a tea set. A rack hung from the ceiling supporting a stainless steel pan set hung on chrome hooks. A large fridge freezer had photographs of the family stuck on with blue tack and there were four pictures on the wall. They were children's drawings that had been framed — one had been done by John and one by Sarah and the other two the twins when they were little. The two done by John and Sarah portrayed people and horses. The twins' pictures were just squiggles in different colours.

'Where's John this evening?' asked Rod.

'He's gone up the Farmer's Arms, there's a quiz night on,' said Mrs Plantington. 'Thank God. When he's home, all he does is go on about Twice a Night and what a waste of money and resources he is.'

'He has got a point; he was hardly a good investment.'

'He keeps calculating how much he costs to feed and stable for a year and waving the figures in front of me.'

'Oh dear me,' said Rod, trying to hold back a smile. John had always been practical and financially minded. He could never understand Mrs Plantington spending her hard-earned cash, and using her time and energy to help sick and dying animals. Rod knew John thought the pair of them were barmy.

'The thing is, I've had an idea. I haven't told John about my plans but as soon as he's better I'm going to stud him out.'

John was taken aback. What a brilliant but simple idea. Why hadn't he thought of it? 'Good thinking Mrs P. Looks like the horse could be a good investment after all.'

Mrs Plantington ladled her soup into two deep pasta bowls and got some crusty bread out of the bread bin. She carved the bread and put it on a plate in the middle of the table. Then she got some fresh butter out of the pantry and put that on the table also. She put a plate of soup in front of Rod then put her own plate on the table and sat down.

Rod ate hungrily; he lived on his own and ate mainly from takeaway joints. He was shy with women and never really met any because he was so busy with his veterinary practice and R.S.P.C.A work. He always envisaged he'd get married and have kids some day. Although he loved Dora, he was aware she was so much older than he and had already had her children. Where he was going to meet his dream women he'd no idea. If she walked into Mrs Plantington's kitchen right this minute, he probably wouldn't have the courage to ask her out. It was rare he got some home cooking. The soup tasted of peas and carrots and some herbs he couldn't put his finger on. 'This is delicious,' he said truthfully. They both ate and dipped in the buttered crusty bread, the butter melting with the hotness of the soup, forming a yellow 'crust' on the soup's surface. Dora hated formality at the dinner table and liked people to dig in and eat in whichever way pleased them.

When they had finished, Rod rubbed his stomach. 'Hmm, I'm full to bursting,' he said.

'I've got some recovering hedgehogs in the animal enclosure,' said Dora. 'They'd been poisoned with something but they are well on the road to recovery now. I'm going to release them in the wild on Friday. Would you like to come and watch, like you used to Rodney?'

'I'd love to,' said Rod, sipping his whiskey, 'but I have to go and inspect Farmer Haywood's cattle on Friday.'

'Oh, that's all right then. I'll do it on my own. I'd ask John or Sarah to come and watch but they wouldn't be interested.,

'I know John wouldn't want to watch, he thinks we're barmy, but wouldn't Sarah like to watch? I remember she used to come with us some times when she was little and release wild birds and stuff. I have a vivid memory of her carrying a pigeon out into the woods and then letting it go, and getting all tearful as she waved it goodbye.'

'No, she's into horses these days and that's it. As far as Sarah's concerned, wild animals are dangerous — they bite, peck and scratch and they have fleas. She's not in the least bit interested in the animal hospital. Neither of them are, they both think I'm bonkers I'm afraid.'

'That's a shame.'

'I know. I like having someone else there to release the animals with, share the moment. Ted used to come with me sometimes before he passed on, God bless his soul. You know, I swear sometimes I can sense Ted behind me, or by my side. I find myself talking to him sometimes. You probably think I'm batty but maybe Ted will come with me.'

'I don't think you're batty Mrs P. There have been times when I've felt my parents' presence. Like when I passed my degree. I could have sworn I could feel them watching over me and I had the feeling they were really proud. There was one time I was leaning on the bridge in Farmer Haywood's bottom field. One of the wooden poles gave way and I nearly fell in the river. I felt someone pull me back. I could swear it was Dad.'

'I always feel like Ted is there when I start getting upset or feeling down. It's like he pops by to cheer me up a bit.'

'I'm not sure if I believe in the afterlife or not,' said Rod, still sipping his whiskey. 'It might just be an overactive imagination because you really miss somebody; you sense them as being there. However, if believing Ted is watching over you brings you some comfort, I'm certainly not going to mock.'

'You know,' said Dora. 'Personality wise, you're more like me than either John or Sarah. It's strange isn't it? I daren't tell John. I can feel his Dad's presence sometimes. He'd call a psychiatrist out for me before you could blink.'

'I'm sure he wouldn't,' said Rod. 'He might laugh a bit and call you a dotty old mare, but I don't think he'd call a head shrink.'

'He would, I swear he would.'

'Anyway, Mrs P. If you'll excuse me, I have to go now,' said Rod, putting the empty glass down on the table. 'I've got an early start in the morning.' He stood up and pushed his chair in.

Dora walked to the door with Rod and he turned round and kissed her. Then he pushed her backwards onto the dining room table and made love to her. He hadn't much experience with women and he fumbled and was finished with quite quickly. Still, the love and respect they felt between each other made up for his lack of sexual technique. Rod felt like crying sometimes when he was making love to her. He felt like he was taking some kind of goddess. That's what she was to him — a goddess. He finished and fastened his pants, grinning. 'Bye Mrs P,' he said, a hint of shyness in his voice. He waved as he got into his Land Rover. 'I'll pop back in a couple of days,' he said, 'to see how the horse is doing. Bye for now Mrs P, take care.'

Chapter Eleven Supermarket Shopping

It was a fine morning. Sunil slept soundly. The doorbell rang. Sunil came running downstairs in his pyjamas and answered the door. It was Julie.

'Hi Julie, I'm sorry I appear to have overslept,' said Sunil apologetically, sweeping his hair back from his face with his hand. 'I thought I had set the alarm but it didn't go off.'

He was lying — he had pressed the snooze button five times. He still felt exhausted from last night's lack of sleep.

'Don't worry,' said Julie. 'It's always playing up that thing.'

'Listen, I'll get the boys up and dressed first then I'll sort myself out. Why don't you make yourself a drink?' said Sunil, yawning and wiping the sleep from his eyes.

'Oh thank you, I will.'

Sunil went back upstairs and Julie went into the kitchen. She put the kettle on then got two bowls out and poured cereal and milk into them. She took them into the dining room and put them on the table. Then she finished making four coffees and went and sat in the lounge and put Breakfast Television on. The twins came down the stairs into the living room, one by one. They walked into the dining room, sat at the table and started to eat their breakfast.

'Good morning!' said Julie. 'Sleep well?'

The twins looked up from their breakfast and nodded. They weren't going to risk speaking to Julie in case Sunil overheard. A few minutes later, Sunil came downstairs.

'Hello Sunil, I've made you a coffee,' Julie said.

She sighed. It was going to be a hard day. The twins were bound to play up with a new staff member on duty. Julie thought it might be easier on her if they split up for the day and took one twin each.

'Thanks,' said Sunil.

The twins finished eating and came through to sit on the couch.

'Today we have to get some money out of the twins' account,' explained Julie. 'We need to pay some bills and do the shopping. If you don't mind, I think it would be easier if I took out one of them and you stayed here with the other one. Okay?'

'Yes, whatever you normally do. You say the boys speak sometimes?' Sunil queried.

'Yes?

'I got them to speak last night. Watch this!'

Sunil started jumping up and down. 'Yes! Yes!' he shouted.

The boys started staring at their fingernails, looking very bored. Sunil jumped up and down again. 'Yes! Yes!'

The twins totally ignored him.

'Yes, well, we'd better be going!' said Julie. 'Come on Harry.'

Harry didn't move. Julie sighed, grabbed hold of Harry's hand and pulled him off the couch. Harry stood up.

'I don't believe this,' said Sunil. 'They copied me last night.'

'I believe you Sunil,' said Julie, full of sympathy for the man. 'One thing you can't accuse the twins of is consistency. I'll see you later.'

Julie and Harry left the house and walked up the road to the bus stop. The bus arrived and Julie and Harry got on it. Julie paid the bus driver and they sat behind two ladies who gossiped away merrily in the way so no one else could understand who they are on about.

'Well, you know who I'm on about — him. You know, I told you he was going out with that girl — you know whom I'm on about. Well, I heard she's pregnant.' The lady that spoke had a blue rinse. She wore a twinset with pearls; a frilly underskirt could be seen under her calf-length skirt. She clasped her hands under her bosom as she spoke.

'She never is?' said the younger lady her eyes wide with disbelief. She sported a floral summer frock and sandals, and a brown shoulder-length hair perm.

'Yes really,' continued the older lady. 'Anyway, I saw someone else in the post office — she told me. You know whom I mean. Not that she's got room to talk; she's sleeping with the pop man. Did I tell you I saw her invite him in, the pop man? A good twenty minutes he was in her house. You're not telling me it took her twenty minutes to pay the man. She thinks everybody's daft. She must realise people are watching her. I'm sure she's sleeping with the window cleaner as well. He always pops inside for a good half hour or so when he goes round to take his money. Anyway, as I said, the other one, you know who I mean; I heard she got herself pregnant. I wonder what she's going to do. Do you think she'll tell his wife on him? Do you think she'll dob him in and claim child support off him? She's only sixteen as well, the dirty little bugger. Imagine sleeping with the babysitter. Dirty bugger! Ey, did I tell you about the other day? I spent ages ironing my daughter's new blouse. I couldn't get the creases out. I kept spraying it with water. Eventually, I managed it and then when she came in she went mad. It was supposed to be crinkled apparently,' she laughed. 'Kids are supposed to look like nobody owns them.' She laughed again. 'Oh look, that's our stop.' The ladies got off the bus, still talking.

'Thank God they've gone,' said Harry.

'Harry! That's not nice,' said Julie.

'Still, they were giving me a headache.' There was nothing Harry hated more than gossipy women going on and on about stuff. It made his brain feel like it was being gripped with a vice; shrill, piercing women's voices going on and on without pausing for breath. Sometimes you got them on the scheme; they could just sit for hours and hours gossiping. Harry wondered how they thought of so many things to talk about. It was never about anything particularly interesting to listen to either. It was always boring stuff about who was seeing who and how much ironing and nappy changing they'd done on their weekend off.

The bus stopped again in the High Street.

'Come on,' said Julie. 'This is our stop.'

Both Julie and Winston got off the bus. They started walking along the High Street, getting jostled by the crowds of people.

'Harry, why did you do that to Sunil?' said Julie suddenly; she hated it when the twins did things to embarrass people. It also annoyed her how they acted like they had severe learning difficulties in front of everyone else. They acted so 'normal' when she was alone with them. 'He seems like a really nice man,' she added.

Harry laughed and rubbed his hands together. Julie growled from the back of her throat.

Town was buzzing. The high street moved with a hoard of people all walking at the same fast-paced speed. A little ahead was an old lady, Harry noticed, with a walking stick that wasn't going with the flow. She kept getting pushed and jostled as people hurried to get past her. She kept stopping and looking irritated over her shoulder before toddling on another few steps. Harry felt a hand on his back. It was a teenager on roller skates. He pirouetted through the crowds, touching people to change direction as he weaved in and out, whizzing past the crowds. The cars were bumper-to-bumper and the air was heavy with petrol fumes drifting nauseatingly in the heat. Car horns peeped and people leant one arm out of their car windows, becoming impatient and tapping their fingernails on the roofs of their cars. Some kids did a moony at the back window of a car, causing their mum to turn round and shout. Eventually, they reached the cash point

'Come on now Harry. I've shown you what to do,' said Julie. Harry keyed his number in. 'You need twenty-five pounds for your monthly gas, twenty-one pounds for your electricity bill, and seventy-six weekly rent; that's one hundred and twenty-two pounds you need to draw this week.'

Harry keyed in the appropriate amount and it was delivered. Across the road, inconspicuous in the crowd, Mrs Plantington was watching and smiling. She'd seen him before many times with Julie, when he didn't know she'd been there. She'd seen him shopping with her in the supermarket, heard him talking to her. She wondered why the twins acted so normal when Julie was there, yet acted daft in front of everyone else. Still, she didn't let on when she visited them that she knew their secret. She'd always suspected they were both brighter than they let on to people. Seeing them with Julie just confirmed her suspicions. She was a bit hurt that they acted so normal in front of Julie and yet acted daft in front of her, their own mother. She wondered what was going on in their heads that made them behave that way. Still, she was pleased that someone was getting through to them, even if it wasn't her.

Harry and Julie went into the post office to pay their bills. They joined the queue. Harry was well-behaved and stood shuffling his feet, watching the car insurance advert on the video screen. A child swung on the ropes that divided the queues of people. Harry wondered whether he should join in but decided against it. After paying the bills, Harry and Julie walked on down the road into the supermarket. Harry grabbed a supermarket trolley, and they started walking on down the aisle. Julie looked at the ready meals on display. 'Hmm, we could get some of these to put in the freezer,' she said.

Behind Harry were packets of cakes. He tapped Julie on the shoulder and pointed at the cakes. 'Can I get some cakes?' he asked.

'Yes, get some if you like,' replied Julie. 'Hmm... lasagne. You all like that don't you? Or what about chicken tikka masala, hmm…?' She put a finger to her lip in concentration. Julie picked up a family size lasagne and turned round to see the trolley was full of packet cakes. She put her hand on her hip and glared at Harry, her face like thunder waving the frozen lasagne in the air with the other hand. Harry put two packets back on the shelf. Julie did not move. Harry put them all back except for four packets and looked at Julie for approval. Julie forced a smile then walked past him briskly. Harry followed with the trolley.

Back at the house, Sunil jumped up in the air

shouting, 'Yes!' Winston copied him shouting, 'Yes!' as he jumped off the sofa. Just then the doorbell rang. Sunil went and answered the door. It was Julie and Harry with the shopping.

'The taxi driver helped us carry the stuff to the front door,' said Julie. 'Could you help us carry it through to the kitchen, Sunil please?'

'Certainly,' said Sunil.

He picked up a couple of bags and took them through to the kitchen. Just then, Michael arrived in his baby blue Rover Estate. He got out of the car and set his alarm by remote control. He stepped over the bags in the hallway and walked into the living room.

'Is there a cup of tea going?' he asked.

'I'll make everyone a cup of tea,' said Sunil, a bit annoyed. Michael could see they were bringing the shopping in and were busy. Not only did he not offer to help, he wanted a cup of tea making, he thought to himself.

The twins were both sat on the sofa. Julie contemplated asking them to help bringing the bags in but decided against it. There was no way they would help her with Sunil and Michael here — that was too much of a normal thing to do. She continued bringing the bags in off the front doorstep, into the kitchen by herself.

'Have we got a replacement for Joan yet?' asked Julie as she walked past Michael with the shopping.

'I'm afraid not,' replied Michael. 'I do wish people wouldn't decide in between shifts that the job isn't for them. Anything could have happened to the twins.'

'What about Nigel?' asked Julie. 'When's he coming back?'

'I don't know, but don't worry; we've managed to

cover the shifts with the agency.'

Julie sighed and started putting the shopping away in the cupboard. She smiled at Sunil.

Harry and Winston looked at each other knowingly and a smile spread across their faces. There was nothing they liked better than winding agency staff up.

Chapter Twelve Agency Staff

The twins were sat on the floor. A man with a short beard and moustache and a number two shaved head was sat cross-legged, also on the floor, playing the guitar. His name was Chris and he wore jeans and a white t shirt with a leather waistcoat over the top.
'Kumbaya my Lord!' he sang to his audience of the two twins. He had always dreamt of getting a gig and singing in public. In the meantime, he took his guitar everywhere with him and got it out at every opportunity. 'Kumbaya my Lord , Kumbaya,' he sang. He knew other songs of course, but he wasn't sure his heavy metal music was appropriate for a supported housing scheme. And anyway, he didn't have his amplifier with him. His usual stuff sounded better on his electric model.

The twins sat silently, studying their fingernails. They wished he would shut up and put the television on. Still, they supposed it was a bit of an honour to be treated to a private performance, so they stayed reverently quite for him and didn't interrupt. When he'd finished, he made the Makaton sign for milk. The twins nodded and he went into the kitchen to get them a glass of milk each. The twins decided they liked him, despite the fact they had missed football on the television.

-----*--------------*-------------*--------------*------

The agency lady, Susan, had been there for about an hour before her mobile went off. She had been reading up on Harry and Winston's case notes. It was her husband on the phone.

'Yes they seem fine,' she said, holding her mobile to her ear. 'I bought a video on the way to work for our Sarah. It's her favourite. It will keep her amused while I do the housework. Do you know, I bet it'll work for these lads as well. Well, they've got learning difficulties. Anyway, I better go love. I'll see you tomorrow around three o'clock.'

The lady stood the men up off the couch. 'Come on you two, stand up a minute,' she said.

She pushed the couch right up to the television and then sat the two men down again. She put a video on. It was *Teletubbies*. She then got the vacuum out and disappeared upstairs with it.

The two men looked at each other and shrugged.

'What the hell is this?' said Harry astounded. 'Is she mad?'

'I think so!' agreed Winston. This video was obviously meant for tiny babies. What was she thinking of? they both thought.

'That explains it then!' Harry looked at Winston and laughed.

'What are they? They look like big talking cushions.'

'I don't know, but it looks like fun dressing up like that.'

'Have you ever wondered what's inside a cushion?' said Winston, picking a cushion up. This staff would have to pay treating them like babies.

'Yes actually,' said Harry.

He picked a cushion up, put his hand inside and pulled out all the little foam pieces, throwing them in the air. Winston followed suit with another pillow.

'Was there anything apart from foam in yours?' asked Winston.

'No,' replied Harry.

'What else can we look inside?' asked Winston.

Both of them got up off the couch and started wandering round the house.

'Look!' said Harry. 'The lady's bag, we can look inside that.'

They found some wool inside the bag. They wound the wool round the dining room chair legs. Then they found some hand cream, which they squirted all over the carpet. The lady's purse was in there as well so they emptied the coins all over the floor along with the empty purse.

'Look,' said Harry 'Chanel No. 5.' They sprayed both of themselves and the room with perfume before throwing the empty bottle in the fish tank along with her hair brush. They found some lipstick and put some on untidily round their lips and halfway up their cheeks before scrawling on the windows with it. They did the same with the kohl stick. Then they sat back down and turned the video off. Taking it out of the video recorder, they pulled the tape out and threw it on the floor. Then they put the news on. The twins liked keeping up to date with current affairs. Maybe they thought they had gone over the top but that lady had severely insulted them. They hated being treated like babies, even although most of the time they acted like small children. They still hadn't grown up; this was their problem. Some may say it's too late to grow up at thirty-something.

----------*--------------*---------------*------------*-------

It was dark and the twins were sat outside on the patio set with their coats on. A man called Simon stood having a cigarette. The man had heard from the previous agency staff member about what a mess the twins had made whilst she was upstairs cleaning, so he was taking no chances. He brought the twins outside with him whilst he had a cigarette. He decided his bladder was full so he took a leak in the outside drain. No chance he was leaving them to go upstairs to the toilet. The twins watched intently. The man had not spoken a word to them since he came on duty. He had just led them about from chair to chair. They had eaten fish fingers and chips for tea. He hadn't even given them a knife and fork; he had just presumed they would be using their fingers. The twins didn't like being treated like they were stupid, even though they acted that way most of the time. Why hadn't he given them a knife and fork? Okay, yes, they were always using their fingers but that was just to wind the staff up. They could use a knife and fork. He could have given them the option instead of presuming they would be using their fingers this evening.

'Venus is shining bright tonight isn't it?' said Winston. 'What a perfect, cloudless night.'

The man looked at Winston, astonished. 'What did you say?'

Winston and Harry proceeded to make moaning and groaning noises, rocking backwards and forwards and wriggling their fingers in front of their faces.

'That shocked him,' signed Harry.

'Did you like that?' signed Winston.

'Mmm,' replied Harry.

The man looked at his cigarette.

'What are they putting in these things these days?'

He put out his cigarette and led Harry and Winston back into the house.

ACTING DAFT

----*----------------*----------------*-------------*-------

The twins were sat on the couch. A lady, Claudette, was sat on chair with her eyes closed. She wore a long flowing floral skirt with an ethnic type cheesecloth-embroidered top. Her long golden hair was held back with a hair band. The light was off and an oil burner and some candles were lit. Enya was playing. 'Sail away, sail away…' The tape finished. The lady opened her eyes. 'Okay you two, time for bed,' she said, feeling the twins would be sufficiently relaxed now to go to sleep.

The twins looked at her incredulously. It was only half past nine and they hadn't watched any television yet this evening. The lady had showered them early, put them into their pyjamas then spent some time rubbing aromatherapy oils into their hands and feet. It was, admittedly, very nice and all that but they'd missed the football. Claudette stood in front of the boys and said very slowly and deliberately 'Time… for… bed,' at the same time making the Makaton hand signal for bed.

The twins just stared at her.

She repeated herself. 'Time for bed,' again making the Makaton sign.

Winston nearly burst out laughing but instead he made some groaning noises and wriggled his fingers in front of his face.

'There's no way we're going to bed yet — it's far too early.'

'I know,' signed Harry. 'I'm not tired, are you?'

Hmm, thought Claudette. 'I know. Harry, come on, get up.' She took his hand and he stood up. 'Stand up Winston. Now, Winston, put your hands on Harry's hips,' she said, standing Winston behind Harry and guiding his hands into place. 'Now, Harry, put your hands on my hips,' she said, standing with her back to Harry whilst guiding his hands into place. Harry looked quizzically over his shoulder at Winston. What was she up to now?

'Ready?' she said. 'Chuff-a-train, chuff-a-train,' she said, shuffling forwards. 'Come on boys! Chuff-a-train, chuff-a-train, we're going to bed.'

She reached the stairs and opened the door. Both boys were dying to burst out laughing but resisted the urge.

'Chuff-a-train, chuff-a-train takes you bed,' she said, climbing the stairs. 'Chuff-a-train; chuff-a-train up the stairs takes you to bed.'

They reached the twins' bedroom and she pulled back the bedclothes. The twins got in bed and Claudette sighed in relief. She tucked them up then made her way to the staff sleep-in bedroom. She took her top off and folded it neatly on the chair. She suddenly had the strangest sensation that somebody was watching her and she turned round to see the twins standing in the doorway.

'Oh no,' she shrieked, grabbing her top and putting it back on quickly. 'Oh please go on back to bed, I'm exhausted.' She ushered them out of the sleep-in room. The boys walked down the corridor and back down the stairs.

'Oh no,' said Claudette, following them. 'Don't you go back downstairs.'

The twins went back down into the front room and sat back on the sofa.

'Nice boobies,' signed Harry.

'Yes, indeed,' signed Winston.

Claudette was at her wits' end. She was

exhausted and wanted to go to bed. She had another piece of inspiration. She went into the kitchen and got two biscuits. She came back into the front room and stood by the stairway door, waving them. 'Come on boys — biscuits. Nice biscuits.'

There was no response from the boys whatsoever.

'Oh what am I going to do?' sighed Claudette, coming back into the room and sitting on the chair. She looked towards the fish tank. The big black carp stared back her with bulging eyes, blowing kisses. 'Oh I give up,' she sighed, eating the biscuits.

Twelve o'clock came around. Claudette had given in to her exhaustion and had fallen asleep and was snoring softly on the chair. Harry looked at Winston. 'Is it time for bed?' he whispered.

'Yes,' replied Winston. They both got up and went upstairs to bed.

------------------*--------------*-------------*--------

Bob was the next to arrive. He had taken them on an outing to the off licence. The twins sat drinking lager. The agency staff Bob was sat drinking lager as well. This is what he had described as a lads' night in. Canned lager and a porno film he had hired from the video shop. 'Treat for you tonight lads,' he had said, winking. 'I'm sure you lads have needs like everybody else.' The twins watched as the naked busty beauties bounced across the screen. They both felt something stir within their trousers. Julie wouldn't approve of this, they both thought. Then the man got up to go to the toilet.

'Quick,' said Winston.

Harry got up and poured lager all over the man's chair.

'If he wasn't wet before, he will be now,' said Winston.

Both of them sniggered, making snot bubbles that they wiped away with their sleeves.

It wasn't like they weren't enjoying the video. It's just, you know. Well, for one, they knew they were never going to get that sort of fun and they were jealous. As for number two… you have to have some fun, haven't you?

Bob came down the stairs and slumped back in his chair. It was a couple of seconds before he noticed the wetness seeping through his trousers.

'Bastards,' he muttered under his breath, jumping up. The twins looked at him innocently as he went back upstairs to get changed.

----------*----------------*----------------*-------------*------

Claudette and Susan were on shopping duty. They got the twins seated on the bus, each one near the window with Claudette and Susan near the aisle.

'So, how are you finding the twins?' asked Susan.

'Hard work,' said Claudette. 'I couldn't get them to bed the other night. I tried everything but they wouldn't go. I was exhausted.

'I can't get them to go to bed either,' said Susan, putting her hand on the dividing rail between the seats and leaning forward.

Harry didn't like being talked about as if he wasn't there so he started making 'urgh urgh' noises and jumping up and down on the seat.

'I fell asleep downstairs on the chair and woke up with a stiff neck,' said Claudette. 'Be quiet Winston, or is it Harry? I get mixed up.'

'Don't know. Me too,' replied Susan.

Winston joined in making 'urgh, urgh' noises and they both started rocking frantically backwards and forwards on their seats, wriggling their fingers in front of their face.

'They're talking about us as if we're not here,' said Winston.

'I know,' said Harry.

Claudette put her hands on Harry's legs to try and stop him from moving. 'Be quite Winston. Stop it both of you.'

Susan tried to pull Winston's hands from in front of his face. 'Be quiet Harry, stop being silly. Oh, I had right problems with them the other night. You should have seen the mess they made when I was upstairs cleaning.'

The twins made noises and rocked and were silly all the way to their bus stop, with the driver watching them exasperatedly through his rear view mirror. 'Can you not keep those two under control?' he said.

'You try,' said Claudette.

They reached their stop. They stood up no problem when the ladies asked them to and walked quietly down to the supermarket, each holding a lady's hand.

'What are we going to do now?' said Claudette. 'Who's going to push the trolley?

'I don't know,' said Susan. 'It's a pity we haven't got wheelchairs we could strap them into — then we could use two wheelchair trolleys. That would keep them in one place as well. I'm scared they're going to try to run off how are we going to stop them?'

In response, the twins started jumping up and down and pulling on the arms of the care staff. They didn't like being spoke about.

'I don't know,' said Claudette. 'Here, I'll take both the twins, you grab a trolley. Claudette took both the twins and Susan grabbed a shopping trolley. They walked in the supermarket. The twins looked at each other and broke free of Claudette. They started fetching various items off the shelves and piling them in the trolley.

'Please make them stop it,' said Susan. 'What are they doing?'

The boys where just picking up anything they could off the shelves and piling it all in the trolley. Susan just stood there aghast with her hands around her face. Some of the other shoppers stopped to stare. 'Stop them Claudette!' shrieked Susan.

'How?' asked Claudette, who had blushed bright red from all the attention. 'Winston, Harry, stop it.'

Claudette went running over to try and grab the twins' hands. They ran off shrieking. She went running after them and chased them round the supermarket. Susan surveyed the scene and burst into tears.

'That's it!' she said between sobs. 'I'm not doing any more shifts with this pair of idiots.' When Claudette caught up with them, both men where laid on the floor doing the dying fly, that is, lying on their backs paddling their arms and legs in the air. They used to like the children's Saturday morning programme TISWAS. Eventually, after lots of pleading, the men got up and all four went home — minus the shopping.

----*-------------*--------------*-------------*---------

ACTING DAFT

It was Friday; pub night. Simon and Bob took them out to a karaoke evening. Various drunken people kept getting up and singing. Harry thought what a noise they were making — he would much rather be at home watching the television. The karaoke stopped and the disco started up. Bob went to the bar. He came back with a tray of drinks and two packets of crisps, which he opened and put in front of the twins.

'Have you ever heard the twins speak?' said Simon.

'Nope,' said Bob. 'I don't think they can speak.'

'I could have sworn one of them said something the other day.'

'What did they say?'

'Can't remember now.'

'I know they can tip drinks over chairs, but I didn't think they could speak.'

Harry and Winston didn't like being talked about. They started making 'urgh, urgh' noises.

'What's up with them now?' asked Simon.

'Don't know,' said Bob. 'Calm down the pair of you.'

Just then, the karaoke started up again. It was some women. 'I believe the children are our future, teach them well and let them lead the way,' she shrieked in a high-pitched nasal voice.

'It's no use,' signed Harry. 'I can't stand this assault on my eardrums any longer. I've got to get out of here.' Harry stood up suddenly, purposely knocking the table over but making it look like it was an accident. The table keeled over towards the two care workers, the opened crisps sliding off the table with the four drinks that were on the table all landing on their laps. Bob and Simon sat gawping at them, mouths open. Both of their trousers were soaked in spilled drinks and covered in soggy crisps.

Winston clapped his hands together and let out a solitary, 'Ha.'

Harry sat down again, his face deadpan as if nothing had happened. Some of the punters started staring but the lady singer was undaunted and carried on like a cats' chorus.

'Well,' said Bob. 'I think you better take the twins outside. I'll call a taxi cab.'

---*---------------*--------------*-------------*-------

The man with the guitar was back. It seemed as if he only knew one song.

'Someone's crying Lord, Kumbaya,' he crooned, 'someone's crying Lord, Kumbaya, someone's crying Lord, Kumbaya, oh Lord, Kumbaya.'

Harry laughed. 'Hee hee.'

Then he clapped once. He felt the man deserved some applause after all the effort he was putting in

'Thank you,' said Chris.

Chapter Thirteen Team Meeting

Julie, Michael, Nigel and Iris sat round an oval table in the scheme's head office. It was the only thing in the room apart from a spring water dispenser and an overhead projector. Various team building posters filled the walls. It was a nice, warm summer's day. The sun streamed in through the window, the light collecting dust particles that swarmed about in the air. Nigel suddenly got a tickly cough; he hacked and hacked then got up and went over to the spring water dispenser and helped himself to a glass. 'Sorry about that everybody,' he said.

Julie stared wistfully out of the window, watching a squirrel as it ran up a tree trunk. The birds could be heard twittering outside as they darted about between the treetops. A colourful array of summer flowers filled the borders; pansies, forget-me-nots, geraniums and miniature roses. Bees buzzed about, busily pollinating the bright and colourful flowers. A red admiral butterfly spiralled down and perched on the window ledge. Julie suddenly became aware that Michael was speaking so she turned her attention to him.

'The mattress on the sleep-in bed has springs showing through, causing injuries to staff members. Now! I've looked into this. The mattress can be replaced but it has to be paid for by the twins. Julie, can you be responsible for buying a new mattress?'

'Yes I suppose so,' she said, tapping the fingernails of one hand on the desk. The other hand was holding up her head; her elbow on the desk, she looked thoroughly bored with the proceedings.

'So that's the minutes from the last meeting. Has anybody any other business?' asked Michael, as if he cared.

'Yes, when are we getting another staff member to replace Joan?' asked Nigel. He was sick of having agency staff leave all the work for him when he came on duty.

'As soon as possible. We are having difficulties finding someone suitable.'

'You said that ages ago,' said Nigel getting heated. 'It really is not good enough. The twins need consistency of care.' He knew the twins played up for new staff much more than for the regular members of staff.

'We've put another advert in the paper,' reassured Michael. 'We'll be interviewing in a couple of months' time.' Michael wasn't as hopeful as he sounded. It really was hard work trying to find anybody with any experience. If you took people on, with no experience that didn't realise what they were letting themselves in for, you risked losing them mid-shift. As happened with Joan.

'What about Sunil?' asked Julie. 'I know the boys like him, can't we take him on?' Julie liked Sunil as well with his deep brown eyes and dark skin and shiny black hair that fell flatteringly around his face.

'Unfortunately, as you must know, Sunil only works part-time,' said Michael. 'Plus, if we took him on we would have to buy him off the agency. Our budget doesn't stretch to that. Sorry.'

'The twins need people they know and trust looking after them. This really isn't good enough. Who's looking after them today?' asked Nigel.

'Sunil,' replied Julie.

'Hmm, he seems nice enough,' said Nigel. 'I've taken handover from him, but never actually worked with him for a full shift. I'm on shopping duty with him this afternoon. If we could fill Joan's place, Sunil could cover sickness and annual leave. We wouldn't need to keep using one-off agency workers.'

'We are trying our best to find someone suitable,' said Michael, stroking his chin.

'Really, there must be something you could do?' asked Nigel.

Just then, the phone started to ring in the main office. Iris, who was taking the minutes of the meeting, put her pad and paper down on the desk. She already knew who it was; she had asked a friend to ring her at half past two. She had supposed Michael would have had enough of the meeting by then.

'Iris, could you get that please,' said Michael, furtively winking as he spoke.

Iris went into the back office. Michael watched her bum wriggle as she walked out of the room. Iris really was a fine figure of a woman, and so attentive. She would do anything for him, he was sure of it. Michael wished that his wife would fawn all over him and pay him as much attention as Iris did. She returned and popped her head round the door.

'Mr Fenchurch, I'm afraid there's a problem at one of the houses,' she said, smiling at Mr Fenchurch and holding his gaze.

'Oh dear, didn't you tell them I'm in a meeting?' replied Michael, smiling back.

'Yes, but it's an emergency.'

'An *emergency* you say. Oh well, I'm afraid I'm going to have to cut this meeting short. We'll arrange another one for six months' time.'

Michael got up and went into the back office. Nigel and Julie looked at each other knowingly. Everybody on the scheme was getting sick of this 'emergency' routine. They stood up and got their coats on to leave.

Later that afternoon, Nigel, Sunil, Harry and Winston where in the supermarket, doing the shopping.

'Sunil, would you mind pushing the trolley?' asked Nigel.

'Of course I don't mind,' replied Sunil.

Sunil took a trolley. Nigel took the groceries list out of his pocket.

'Harry, you get the lettuce and cucumber please!' ordered Nigel. 'Winston, tomatoes and beetroot please.'

The twins went over to the salad section, got the items and put them into in the trolley.

'They certainly know their grocery items, don't they?' observed Sunil.

'They certainly do,' confirmed Nigel.

'Have you ever heard them speak?' asked Sunil.

'No, never,' replied Nigel.

'We were watching football the other day,' said Sunil, 'and I jumped up and said yes when Man United scored and the twins copied me and they said yes too.'

'Really?' said Nigel. 'Julie told me they speak sometimes, but I've never heard them, not a dickey bird, and I've worked with them for seven years now.'

'Strange isn't it?' observed Sunil. 'I mean, they won't do it when anyone else is listening.'

'Hmm… that's what Julie says,' said Nigel. 'Hmm… strange indeed! Ah well, must get on.'

Nigel walked on ahead and Sunil followed with the trolley.

Sunil still thought there was something odd about the twins; they were different to the other people he had worked with who had severe learning difficulties. Like the fact they knew grocery items and things. The way they only said 'yes' to him when nobody else was listening. He couldn't put his finger on what was wrong with the situation. There was just something strange about them. Like they were mentally ill, rather than having learning difficulties.

'Now,' said Nigel. 'I want you to bring me two loaves of bread each please.'

The twins got the loaves of bread and put them in the basket, and then followed Nigel as he walked on down the aisle with the supermarket trolley.

Chapter Fourteen The Stud

Twelve months had passed. The sun shone brightly, making the warm air shimmer with the heat. Flies and bluebottles buzzed round the neat piles of horse manure in the field. Rabbits hopped about nonchalantly grazing on the grass, twitching their little noses and catching the scent on the air on guard to sniff out any predators. Blackbirds could be heard cawing to each other from high in the branches of the trees where they had made nests out of twigs. They flew down to catch prey to take back to the youngsters in the nests. Buttercups and daisies nodded their heads in the breeze and glinted in the sunlight. Bees buzzed about pollinating the flowers and butterflies gracefully spiralled about on the breeze. Twice a Night was with a mare in a paddock. They were mating. Dora and a farmer watched.

'He won a lot of races, he's a fine horse,' said Dora. 'Okay, he tripped up at that fence, an easy mistake for any horse to make. He was always very fast.'

'You don't need to sell Twice a Night to me, Mrs Plantington,' replied the farmer. 'He was good. No! A brilliant racehorse that made a silly mistake any racehorse could make. You could have said he was just plain unlucky. Then again, he was very lucky you were watching and saved him from death. Personally, I haven't really time for racehorses with the farm and everything. This here mare belongs to my daughter Mary. She looks after her and trains her and everything. She came third in some race last year, won her quite a tidy sum of money so far. Anyway, he's done the deed. There's one thousand pounds. He's a good horse with good genes. His foals should bring a good price.'

Dora went into the paddock, retrieved Twice a Night and led him into the horsebox. She fastened the door shut and hopped into the driving seat of the Land Rover. 'Bye,' she said as she put the keys in the ignition.

'Bye,' said the farmer, waving her off. 'Have a safe journey home.'

The journey home took about an hour and a half. Eventually, Dora pulled into the stables. She got out of the Land Rover, took out Twice a Night and led him toward the stables. Twice a Night started whinnying and pulling on the reigns.

'What on Earth's the matter?' Dora asked the horse, as if expecting a reply.

Twice a Night started pulling towards one of the stables. A mare inside the stable whinnied back to him, rearing up on her hind legs.

'That's Bluebell's stable,' observed Dora. 'Well, you little tinker, fancy your chances do you?'

Dora unlocked the stable and let Twice a Night in. Some whinnying and neighing ensued.

'Well, it looks like the feeling's reciprocated,' said Dora laughing. 'Now I know why they called you Twice a Night. Still, you've made a tidy profit for me in the last few months. I guess I owe it to you. What if she gets pregnant? What do I tell John? Oh well!' Dora started to giggle. John was in for a shock.

The whole team was in the office. Julie, Nigel, Sunil, Claudette, Chris, Nigel and Iris slouched around the table in the meeting room. Julie watched the squirrels and rabbits playing about on the grass outside the office window.

'Now then,' said Michael. 'Nigel asked at the last meeting about getting a computer for the boys and also so the staff can do assessments and so forth on it. The boys can buy one between them but I'm afraid we as a company won't be putting any money towards it. I've checked the boys' saving account. They can afford a basic one and basic printer but that will mean they can't afford to go on holiday this year. Nigel, if you wouldn't mind looking into buying a cheap, basic computer package and also some software the twins will be able to use on it. I'm sure they wouldn't mind the staff using it occasionally if it's being used in their interest.

Now, staffing issues. As you know, we employed Fred but he only lasted a week, slightly longer than Joan but anyway he decided to go back to taxi driving. That leaves us back to the agency staff. Sunil, Claudette and Chris have all been working for us on a regular basis but as I'm sure you're aware we could do with staff employed on the scheme. We've put another advert in the paper and interviews are next week. Hopefully, we'll find somebody suitable amongst the shortlist of candidates but we'll just have to manage until then. Sunil, Claudette and Chris, we're grateful to you for providing some continuity of care. Now, has anybody any other business?'

'Yes,' said Claudette. 'I've been thinking the twins really could do with some sort of skills training. I thought perhaps learning to dress themselves. I know it's a tall order but I thought we could start with something simple like teaching them to put their own socks on. I've gone to the liberty of designing a training programme. What does everybody think?

Suddenly, Julie burst out into the giggles. She knew full well the twins could dress themselves.

'What's the matter Julie?' asked Sunil, his face full of concern.

'Nothing,' said Julie, squealing with laughter. She put her hands over her mouth to try and stop herself from laughing. The twins showered and dressed themselves without any help when she was on duty and Claudette wanted to teach them to put socks on.

'What's the matter?' said Michael. 'Let us all in on the joke.'

'I'm sorry,' said Julie. 'I can't help it.' she said, still shaking with suppressed giggles.

'I don't think Claudette's idea is funny. I think it's a good idea to be doing something constructive with the twins,' said Michael.

'Yes of course it is,' said Julie, coughing and trying to compose herself but it was no use. Her body started shaking again as she desperately tried to stop herself giggling.

'What's got into you Julie?' asked Nigel, giving her a funny look.

'Nothing,' said Julie. 'It's just something funny came into my head, that's all.'

'Well I wish you'd share the joke with all of us,' scolded Michael.

'It's nothing, sorry,' said Julie, flapping her hand. 'Sorry about that everybody.'

'Are you sure you're all right Julie?' said Nigel. 'Is there something bothering you?'

'No, I'm fine honest,' protested Julie. 'Sorry about that — I don't know what came over me.'

'Right,' said Michael. 'That's decided then. Every morning from now on the staff can teach the boys to put there own socks on using Claudette's training programme and we'll record what progress they're making.'

Julie sat, eyes bulging and cheeks sucked in, her

arms folded in front of her chest.

'Are you sure you are all right Julie?' asked Michael. 'You don't look right to me.'

Julie nodded.

The phone rang and Iris went to answer it. Michael watched her bum wriggle as she walked into the back office and he imagined himself stood behind her feeling her buttocks.

She came back into the room and gazed into Michael's eyes. Electricity leapt across the room as they looked at each other. 'Mr Fenchurch,' she said. 'I'm afraid there's an emergency in one of the houses.'

'Oh dear,' said Michael, looking at Iris longingly. 'We will have to bring the meeting to a close. Hopefully, next time we meet in six months we'll have some good news on the staff front.'

Everybody sighed and got up to leave.

Three months had passed and frost hung in the air. The fields where covered in a light dusting of snow. Bluebell was standing in her stable. A vet examined her stomach. John was standing nearby; he shuffled his feet in the hay.

'The groom noticed it when he was brushing her,' he said. 'A lump in her stomach. He said he didn't take much notice at first but it's been getting bigger. What do you think it is? Do you think it's cancer? Oh my God, I hope we don't have to put her down — she's a real favourite with the young girls in the riding school. They all ask for her specially.'

'She's pregnant,' said the vet. 'I'm surprised with your experience of horses you didn't work out what the problem was yourself.'

'What?! She can't be pregnant. I mean… we never let her out with any of the stallions — it's impossible! It's absolutely impossible. You must have made a mistake.'

'I've been practising veterinary medicine for twenty-five years,' said the vet. 'I know a pregnant mare when I see one. About three months gone I'd say.'

'But how could this have happened ……?' He paused to think. 'Mother! I'd bet my life she has something to do with this.' Mother was always behind anything strange or unusual that happened at the stables. 'Excuse me Douglas. Maybe I can catch her before she sets off for the twins' party.'

The vet packed up his bag of tricks and made back to his Land Rover as John ran off over to the house.

Chapter Fifteen The Party

The twins sat next to each other on the couch, dressed in their best black suits, with blue shirts and black ties with white Chinese dragons on the front. Michael, Nigel, Sunil, Iris, Chris and Claudette from the agency stood round making polite conversation. The table was laid with sandwiches, sausage rolls, cheese sticks, chicken legs and a bowl of salad. Music was playing. Julie came out of the kitchen with some paper plates and put them on the table. Michael came into the dining room.

'Is the grub ready?' he asked. 'Good, I'm starving.'

'I think we should wait for Mrs Plantington,' said Julie. 'She shouldn't be long. It's not like her to be late.'

Michael went back into the front room were the twins were sat on the settee. Stood round were Nigel, Iris, Claudette and Sunil. Everyone was stood is silence; the conversation having dried up.

'Well, isn't this nice?' said Michael. 'Is everyone having fun?'

'Yes,' said Iris, looking lovingly at Michael.

'Yes,' said Nigel.

'Yes, I'm enjoying myself thank you,' said Sunil.

'Yes, it was so nice of you to invite me,' said Claudette.

'Yes,' said Chris.

'Iris,' said Michael, 'did you have a nice weekend?'

'Not bad,' said Iris. 'I went ice skating with the kids. We had a nice time but I fell over and bruised my bum.'

Iris wondered if she should ask Michael if he

wanted to look at the bruise on her bum but decided against it.

Michael pondered on whether he should ask to see the bruise on her bum but decided against it.

'And you,' said Iris, 'did you have a nice weekend?'

'Not really,' said Michael. 'I've been arguing with the wife again. I can't remember what it was about now but she was really shouting at me — going ballistic. I don't know what it is I keep doing wrong.'

'Oh dear,' said Iris. She bet he'd done nothing wrong. That mad bitch wife of his was always shouting at him for some reason. *She* wouldn't shout at him if he were *her* husband. She'd treat him very nicely indeed. That silly bitch wife of his didn't know she was born being married to someone as nice as Michael. She wanted to be married to her husband — now he really was a lazy, fat so-and-so. She'd have something to complain about then. Iris wished they weren't both already married so she could tell him how she felt.

'Ah well,' said Michael. 'All couples have their problems I suppose.'

He figured life would be easier if he were married to Iris. She didn't shout at him. She didn't argue. She always did what he said first time without speaking back. In fact, she second-guessed what he wanted most of the time. He didn't even need to tell her what he wanted or needed; she already knew. Michael wished they weren't both married so he could tell her how he felt.

The twins start humming and swaying to the music. They were not dead keen on these parties. There were too many staff around to get into any mischief. Still, they decided they might as well get into the spirit of things.

'Well, the twins are certainly enjoying themselves,' said Michael, smiling manically at everyone. 'And, after all, that's why we are here, in honour of the birthday boys.'

An awkward silence prevailed. Everyone started staring at their feet. Julie came in with a bottle of wine and some glasses.

'Wine anybody?' she asked.

Michael, Iris, Chris and Nigel all answer in unison. 'Yes please!'

'I'm fine thank you,' said Claudette.

'Actually, I'm driving,' said Sunil. 'Any chance of a cup of tea please?'

'Certainly there is,' said Julie. 'I'll have one myself as I'm on duty.'

She poured out the wine for Michael, Nigel, Chris and Iris then disappeared into the kitchen. She came back with two lagers on a tray and gave them to the boys. 'There you are boys. The tea won't be a minute. Sunil, I've put the kettle on.'

'Should the boys be drinking lager?' asked Claudette.

'Why should they not?' Julie answered. 'They like a tipple now and again. Anyway, it's their birthday.'

'Won't it interact with their medication?' Claudette persisted.

'What medication?' asked Julie, somewhat bemused.

'Those big black tablets they have to take every morning,' said Claudette.

'Those are iron tablets,' said Julie.

'It says ferrous sulphate on the medication sheet,' Claudette contradicted.

'Like I said,' explained Julie. 'Iron tablets. Ferrous sulphate means iron in posh medical speak.'

'Oh,' said Claudette, flushing bright red.

'Anyway, I don't think the boys will be driving tonight!' interjected Michael 'I've hidden their keys.'

Everybody tittered. The room went silent again apart from the music. Michael looked at his watch then started tapping his foot to the music.

Iris studied Michael's face; he could be so funny sometimes, she thought. He had kind eyes and the most beautiful smile. It always made her feel happy when Michael smiled at her.

The twins looked at each other — they were bored to tears. Harry tried to think of something he could do to liven things up a bit but there were too many staff. They all looked very smart, he thought. Iris was in a blue skirt suit with a pink frilly blouse underneath. Harry always thought she looked like a schoolteacher, the way she had her glasses perched on the end of her nose. Her perfectly manicured nails matched her blouse. Her shoes were exactly the same colour as her suit. Harry swore he had never seen her in the same pair of shoes twice. Not that he saw her that often; she was usually just a voice at the other end of the telephone. He had noticed the way she looked all gooey-eyed at Michael. Michael had come casual this evening in fashionable faded blue jeans and a lose fitting blue shirt, unfastened over a white t-shirt. He had noticed Michael looking at Iris as well. It was like some sort of mutual appreciation society. Sometimes you could feel electricity in the air when they looked at each other.

'Do you think Michael likes Iris?' he signed to Winston.

'Yes and she him,' he signed the reply.

'I wonder if they kiss sometimes,' signed Harry.

'Don't know. They might do when nobody's around,' Winston signed back, smirking.

Then there was Sunil; Harry would have described him as cute. There was a child-like quality about him, something about his soft brown eyes and the way he stood, hands in pockets. Rocking backwards and forwards slightly from toe to heel. Harry could tell Julie liked him although she never did anything or said anything obvious. Julie had got dressed up today. She had black pants on and a shiny aubergine blouse. She had a flower pendant and earrings in; she had even gone as far as some brown eye shadow and pink lipstick. It wasn't often you saw Julie in makeup.

'Do you think Julie likes Sunil?' signed Harry.

'Yes,' signed Winston. 'Her voice goes all funny when she speaks to him.'

Nigel wore checked chinos and a plain white shirt. His neatly cut beard picked out the brown check in his chinos. Nigel, Harry thought, looked like a geography teacher or wildlife expert. He could just imagine him out on the moors with a pair of binoculars, bird watching.

Claudette was dressed in a flowing ethnic skirt and top. She had been to the hairdresser and her hair was now plaited with beads in. Harry wondered if she'd ever been on a Greenpeace march or lived up a tree to stop it being chopped down.

Chris had jeans on and a waistcoat. As usual, his trusty guitar leant against the wall.

Both twins reached for their lager at the same time. They took a swig than sat back and started humming to the music.

'Did anyone see the Man United game on Saturday?' said Sunil, who'd been racking his brains trying to think of something to say to start a conversation off with. ‘It was awesome.’

‘Hmm… no sorry I didn’t,’ replied Michael, looking at Iris.

‘Me neither!’ said Iris, looking at Michael and smiling provocatively.

‘Sorry Sunil I don’t watch football,’ said Nigel.

Silence befell the room again. Julie came in with two cups of tea and gave one to Sunil, keeping the other herself.

‘Thanks Julie,’ said Sunil. ‘Did you watch the Man U game on Saturday?’

‘Yes I watched it with the twins,’ said Julie. ‘That man got a goal, didn’t he? What’s his name now? He’s married to Posh Spice’

‘David Beckham,’ replied Sunil.

‘That’s him!’ said Julie.

‘It was a brilliant goal — the way he dribbled up the left wing past the defender and bang, straight into the back of the net. The goalkeeper didn’t stand a chance. I tell you, I nearly died when Liverpool nearly equalised in the last few minutes. It’s a good job it was offside.

'What’s that then, offside?’ asked Julie

A blank expression washed over Sunil’s face. He looked at the floor and scratched his nose.

‘Oh excuse me,’ he said. ‘This tea’s gone straight to my bladder.’ He put his cup of tea down on the table and disappeared upstairs.

‘So Michael,’ said Nigel. ‘Any news on a new staff member yet?’

‘Oh come on Nigel,’ replied Michael, ‘this is supposed to be a party. We don’t want to talk shop all night. Anybody want to talk shop all night at the twins’ birthday party? Of course we don’t!’

'Here, I've got a joke,' said Julie. 'What do call a deer with no eyes?'

'We don't know,' replied Michael.

'No eye deer,' said Julie, laughing as she spoke.

'I'm sorry. What?' said Michael 'I don't get it.'

'It's a pun,' explained Nigel. 'No idea - no eye deer.'

'Oh I see,' said Michael.

'It's not nice to joke about visually disabled creatures Julie,' Claudette scolded.

Sunil came back down the stairs and picked his cup of tea up off the coffee table. 'Did I miss anything?' he asked.

'Not much!' replied Julie. 'I told a joke but nobody thought it was funny.'

'Oh! I have a joke,' said Sunil. 'I heard it yesterday. There's this guy — he's lonely and broke and has no job. So he gets invited to a wedding of his friend. He is marrying a beautiful wife. Everywhere he goes the other men are talking about the groom and how he deserves a nice wife because he has lots of hope, lots of faith and gives a lot to charity. Anyway, five months later this groom decides to visit his old friend. So he goes round to his house and there are two very big fat ladies sat on his couch. Coming from upstairs can be heard, "Come to me, hurry big boy, I'm waiting for you, come and give it to me." So the groom said, "What's going on?" The man said, "Well, on my way home from your wedding I passed a wishing well so I threw in a coin and asked for lots of faith, lots of hope and to be able to give lots to charity." So the groom says, "yes, so?" So the man says, "Here is faith and hope and upstairs is 92-year-old Charity."'

Julie laughed and the twins sniggered.

The twins signed to each other, ‘Good joke.’

‘Oh I see yes, very clever,’ said Michael.

‘That’s very funny actually. I like that,’ added Nigel

‘That’s not funny at all,’ said Claudette. ‘I’m surprised at you Sunil. I’m leaving. I’ve had enough of this.’

Claudette picked her handbag up off the chair and made for the door. Julie followed, waving to her as she made off down the road. ‘Bye then,’ said Julie. ‘Thanks for coming.’

Julie went back into the living room.

‘Was that something I said?’ asked Sunil.

‘Dunno love,’ said Julie. ‘She’s a strange one. Give us your cup then — I’ll make us another brew.’

‘I think I’ll come with you,’ said Sunil.

Julie and Sunil both went into the kitchen.

'Here, I’ll turn the music off for a second. I’ll play you some nice guitar music,’ said Chris. He turned off the CD player, to everybody’s bemusement, than sat on the floor cross-legged with his guitar. ‘Kumbaya my Lord, Kumbaya…’

Everybody looked at each other; they had to suppress the giggles. They watched their own shuffling feet on the floor, desperately sucking their cheeks in trying not to laugh. Michael looked at his watch again and then popped his head round the kitchen door.

‘Listen Julie,’ he said. ‘It doesn’t look like Mrs Plantington is coming. Is it okay if we start on the food?’

‘I suppose so,’ said Julie. ‘It is getting on a bit. It’s not like Mrs Plantington to be late — something must be wrong.’

‘Great I’m starving,’ said Michael. ‘Nigel! Would you help me fill two plates up for the twins?’

Nigel and Michael filled a plate up each from the buffet and put them in front of the twins. Chris was still singing *Kumbaya* and gave them a bit of a dirty look for starting the buffet in the middle of his recital. The twins start to eat hungrily. Michael went to the table and started helping himself to the food. The other staff members queued up behind him with their paper plates.

'It all looks very nice,' commented Iris. She watched Michael filling his plate up. She loved the way he was so masterful without being aggressive. His bum looked nice and pert in the jeans he was wearing. She made a mental note of what he was putting on his plate in case he ever asked her to get a buffet for him. She wanted to know what he liked.

'It looks lovely, doesn't it?' agreed Nigel.

Everybody filled their plate and went back to the front room to eat. Julie and Sunil came out of the kitchen with their cups of tea and get a plate each. Sunil was in the middle of another joke. 'Anyway then the Scotsman said.........'

Just then, the phone started to ring.

'Oh, excuse me Sunil,' said Julie. 'I better get that,' she said, putting her plate down on the table. Julie picked up the phone.

'Hello? Oh hello, Mr Plantington,' Julie paused, not knowing what to say. 'Oh no, that's terrible. I only spoke to her last week. Well, they'll have to be told. You did right to ring up Mr Plantington. Thank you! Please send my condolences to the rest of the family.'

Julie put the phone down again and walked into the front room.

'I wonder, could we have a conference in the kitchen everybody?' she asked solemnly. The colour had drained from her face and she looked decidedly unwell.

'Certainly,' said Michael, his tone of voice conveying concern.

Chris stopped singing and leant his guitar back against the wall.

Everyone went into the kitchen, taking their buffet plates with them. The twins, still sat on the couch, looked at each other quizzically. They started to whisper to one another. 'What's this all about?' said Harry.

'I don't know,' replied Winston. 'Did you hear anything, the phone call? Did you hear what Julie was saying?'

'No!'

'Maybe there's an emergency in one of the other houses,' suggested Winston.

They both sniggered.

'Shush,' said Harry. "I'm trying to listen!"

The sound of muffled whispers came from the kitchen.

'It's no good,' said Harry. 'I can't hear.'

'Maybe they've run out funding,' suggested Winston.

'Don't be daft,' replied Harry. They both took another swig of lager.

'Well something must have happened to call a team meeting in the middle of a party,' observed Winston, getting a bit flustered.

'Anyway, where's Mum. Why isn't she here yet?' asked Harry.

'That new horse must be poorly again,' surmised Winston.

'Maybe that was Mum' suggested Harry. 'Maybe she wants another racehorse and she's trying to get the staff to form a syndicate.'

'Don't be daft!' said Winston, picking his nose.

'You never know, she might do. Shush they're coming back!'

Michael came out of the kitchen with the others following behind, all of them looking very grave faced.

'Well, I think it's best if we all go now and leave this is your capable hands Julie,' said Michael. 'That was a very nice buffet by the way. Well done!'

All the staff followed Michael to the door, picking up their coats and handbags on the way. Julie grabbed Michael's arm as he was leaving.

'Please don't go Michael; I'm no good at this sort of thing. Couldn't you tell them?' she asked imploringly.

'Nonsense Julie, you'll do fine,' said Michael, pulling away from her grip. 'Anyway, you're closer to the boys than me. It's better to come from someone they know well.'

'Nigel?' asked Julie 'You're close to the boys.'

'Women are more tactful in these situations,' replied Nigel. 'Don't you think Mick?' He stood with his coat over his arm and one hand on the door, waiting for the taxis Michael had called from his mobile phone in the kitchen. He and Iris were sharing.

'I've always found so!' said Michael.

'Don't look at me. I'm just the secretary,' said Iris.

'Well, bye everyone,' said Sunil from the driveway, unlocking his car door.

'Bye,' said Chris, heading off to the bus stop with his guitar over his arm.

The taxis arrived at the back of one another. Nigel got in the front one and Michael and Iris got into the other. Michael couldn't help noticing the fine gold ankle bracelet Iris had on. She had beautiful ankles, he thought. He imagined himself holding her foot in his hand and kissing it gently. He imagined kissing upwards onto her calf… then he had to quickly think of Roy Hattersley again before anyone noticed his excitement.

Julie closed the door and took a deep breath. She went into the front room and sat between Winston and Harry on the couch.

'What's the matter Julie?' asked Winston.

'That was your brother on the phone,' began Julie. 'He went to see your mum earlier and found her collapsed on the floor. He rang an ambulance straight away but, well, she didn't make it. I'm afraid your mum has passed away.'

'Passed where?' asked Harry.

'Your mum's dead, Harry,' said Julie. 'I'm sorry; they think it was a heart attack.'

'No! No!' cried Harry.

He couldn't believe this was really happening. Julie must be making some kind of sick joke. How could she joke about something like this? He took a swing at Julie. Julie ducked and put her hands over her head. Winston stood up and held Harry back.

'It's not Julie's fault Harry. Stop it.'

'I know,' he said in a squeaky voice.

He started crying and put his arms around Winston, who started crying also.

'Mum's dead,' said Harry. 'She can't be. I never told her how much I loved her.'

Suddenly, he started to regret being such a bastard all of his life. He wished they'd never started playing this stupid game but now all his wishing was in vain. Mum was dead and he could never bring her back. Reality was beginning to sink in about what he and Winston had done; were doing to themselves. It was nobody's fault but their own. He started having flashbacks to his childhood days with Mum smiling down on them. Now he would never see the face he loved so much again.

'Me neither,' sobbed Winston. 'It's too late now. Too late to tell Mum now.'

Both of their heads spun. They had never intended to come clean to Mum but now she had died everything seemed so final. They had never spoken to her, not once in all the years of their existence. Now they wished they had. They wanted to tell her how much they loved her. How grateful they both were that she had never given up on them. All those years of teaching them things from books, even though she didn't have any knowledge as to whether her efforts where succeeding. Buying those science and astronomy books, taking them horse riding. Caring for them, looking after them, making them meals, washing their clothes, and generally being there for them in every respect. Words could not convey how much they loved their mother and now she was gone. They would never see her face again. They wished they had said something to her. Told her how much they loved her. Explained to her how much she meant to them, but now it was too late. Much, much, too late.

Harry and Winston were mortified. It was like a hammer had hit them both in the chest and left them with an empty space that could never be filled. They hated themselves for their own deception. Hated themselves for the way they had treated their mother. Now it could never be put right. They would hate themselves forever. They climbed the stairs with heavy limbs, threw themselves on their respective beds and cried themselves to sleep.

Chapter sixteen The Final Goodbye

The churchyard was covered with a fine veil of frost and mist. People were gathered around a coffin in the graveyard. The twins were dressed in black, as were Julie, John, Sarah and Rod, along with several other mourners. The breath of the mourners was visible, turning to mist as they exhaled. People stood rubbing their hands together in the cold and coughing. The vicar spoke:

'Mrs Plantington has been a member of this parish all of her life. She was christened in this very church and was well loved. She always had a great love of animals, she had a great gift of healing, and the villagers often took her injured woodland creatures. Holding a degree in veterinary surgery, she would lovingly restore them to health before returning them to the wild. Her last labour of love was, of course, the racehorse she recently saved from certain death by buying it from the owner just as it was about to be put down. She wasn't just good with animals; she was good with people as well. She raised four fine children, two of whom — the twins — have learning difficulties. She was well loved by them, her late husband and many people who live in the village. She always had a lot of time for people and will be greatly missed by everyone, especially by her four children, John, Harry, Winston, and Sarah. Now she goes to join her late husband Ted, who I'm sure is waiting for her in Heaven. Ashes to ashes, dust to dust…'

Sobbing could be heard as people threw soil and flowers onto the lowered coffin.

Later that afternoon, everybody was back at the stables cottage. They stood mingling in a large room. Inside was a large leather Chesterfield suite, a large piano, a very ornate and antique-looking dresser that had pot horses on it, a large shelving unit that also had pot horses on it and a large pullout table that was laden with a buffet and alcoholic beverages. John was talking to Julie.

'I wasn't sure if the twins would understand, but they do, don't they?' said John.

'Yes, they're inconsolable, Mr Plantington,' said Julie. 'They really loved their mum.'

'As did we all,' said John. 'Despite her little quirks and eccentricities, we all loved her very much. Sarah and I are very grateful to all you care workers for looking after the twins. We know they can be a handful. In fact, they made my life hell when I was a kid. Sarah and I certainly couldn't cope with them, not with the stables as well. It's good to know they are being cared for by professionals.'

Just then, a lady dressed in a black skirt suit with brown hair and crimson cheeks came over.

'John, it's getting on a bit. It's time you read the will out.'

'Oh yes,' said John, looking at his watch. 'You haven't met Julie have you? Mary, this is Julie — the twins' care worker. Julie this is Mary. You'll never believe how we met. Mary rang up wanting that racehorse of my mother's for one of her friends. It appears she's been studding him out without telling any of us. Mary's mare is pregnant by him and she knew somebody else who wanted to hire him as a stud for her horse. I wondered what she was up to, keeping taking him out in the horsebox. Anyway, I told her about Mum passing on and she came straight over to see me and, well, we've been seeing quite a lot of each other recently. In fact, we've been inseparable, haven't we Mary? Anyway, as Mary says, it's time I read the will out. Excuse me.'

'Of course,' said Julie.

John walked over to the other end of the room, rattled a teaspoon against a glass and coughed.

'Can I have your attention please? I would like first of all to thank the vicar for a lovely service.'

Everybody nodded his or her heads in agreement.

'As you all know, you have to be born in the village to be buried in St. Andrew's church. Mother was laid to rest in the same plot as our father, as per her wishes. As her executer, I would now like to read out her will. She makes mention in her will of the fact that the stables were left by our father, in joint names, to herself, Sarah and me. Obviously, her share now passes to Sarah and me, making us both joint owners. Also, the house is to be split equally between Sarah and myself. All of her medicine, herbal healing and animal books have been left to Rod Smith. Five hundred pounds in money, plus her special secret recipe book, go to her best friend, Madge.'

'Oh! I can't believe she left me her recipes, how wonderful,' enthused Madge. 'I've been badgering her for years about her country soup.'

'I'm glad you're pleased Madge,' said John. 'All her clothes, handbags etc. are to be given to charity. Mum's extensive pot horse collection will be auctioned with the proceeds to go to the R.S.P.C.A. Last but not least, the twins. Mother left a letter that she wished me to read out.'

John took the letter out of the envelope and

began to read.

'One of my lasting memories of the twins is how they used to love Ted's old wallet. It was very special to both of us; Ted bought it on our honeymoon. He used to let them play with it. How they used to fight over that wallet. They used to sit for hours just smelling the leather. It's hard to think what the twins would appreciate after my death, but I hope when they smell the leather they remember their Dad and me. I can't think of anybody that would love that old smelly wallet more than them.'

John walked over to Harry and handed him the wallet. 'There you go boys, Dad's old smelly wallet.'

The boys start trying to sniff the wallet and rub it against their faces. Sounds of
'Awe look at that,' and stifled sobs came from the room.

'She knew her boys, didn't she?' commented one mourner.

'Mum also has placed one thousand pounds in their spending money. If you could make sure that goes in a safe place Julie.'

Sobs and sounds of nose blowing filled the room.

'The rest of her money is to be split equally between the twins and Rod Smith,' said John, his voice registering his surprise and shock.

John looked at the will again — this couldn't be right. He looked up at Rod who was sat quietly in a corner, red-faced, tears streaming down his face and rubbing his nose with a tissue. Now was not the right time to make a fuss, thought John, but he was certainly going to contest this. Why should Rod get so much of her money and the twins? They had no use for it. Rod had never done anything for his mother — he and Sarah looked after her, not Rod and the twins. He shuffled his feet nervously. He recovered his composure.

'Also, I found this in Mum's kitchen,' added John. 'It's the twins' birthday present, all wrapped up of course.'

John handed Julie a largish parcel.

'Thanks,' said Julie. 'I think we should wait till we get home to open it.'

'Whatever you think is best. Okay, there's a buffet on the table. Help yourselves to drinks. Try to be happy and enjoy yourselves. That's how Mum would have wanted it.'

Julie and the twins stayed about an hour, the twins getting quite drunk off the wine, which flowed from a huge wine box. The twins noticed John was very friendly with that new Mary lady.

'Have you noticed Mary and John?' signed Harry. 'They've never left each other's side all afternoon.'

John made a joke to her and they both laughed as Winston and Harry watched.

'I wonder if there'll be a wedding soon,' signed Winston. 'And if so, will we be invited?'

'Do you think they've had sex yet?' asked Harry.

'Knowing John's luck, probably,' signed Winston. 'He got a share in the stables.' The twins had been so mortified at not getting a share in the stables, they hadn't heard the bit about them inheriting some money.

Sarah didn't seem to have anybody; she stood talking to two of the female stable hands. Still, at least she had friends. Harry and Winston just had each other and that was all. Most of the time it was enough but sometimes — like at the party — they wished they could join in with the conversation. They had Julie of course. However, it would be nice to have other friends they could talk to, have a laugh with. Harry and Winston had pangs of jealousy. Jealous of John having a girlfriend, who he might be having sex with, jealous of Sarah having friends, jealous of both Sarah and John inheriting the stables, when all they got was a wallet and one thousand pounds between them. They hadn't heard John say she'd left them her money. If anybody knew they could speak, they would have made a drunken fuss. As it was, they just ate the sandwiches, drank the wine and then Julie made their excuses and they left. They stood up, the floor spinning, and staggered out to the car.

Julie pulled up outside the twins' house; Winston was sat in the back with the present on his knee. Harry was sat in the front holding the wallet.

'Are you okay Harry?' asked Julie.

'Yes,' replied Harry solemnly. He wasn't really — he felt confused, sad, angry and drunk. He certainly didn't feel okay.

All three got out of the car. Julie opened the door with her key. The twins went straight upstairs to their room. Julie went into the front room. Nigel was there, sat watching television with a big mug of coffee.

'How are the boys?' asked Nigel.

'Not good,' replied Julie. 'They're both really upset. I think they've gone straight to bed.'

'I wasn't sure if they would understand,' said Nigel. 'You know, about death.'

'Yes, well, if you don't mind,' said Julie. 'I think I will go home now. I'm quite upset myself. I've never seen the twins like this.'

'Of course,' replied Nigel.

'Oh, I nearly forgot,' said Julie. 'Harry has a wallet. His mum left it to them. It has one thousand pounds inside so you might want to put it in the safe.'

'Of course,' said Nigel. 'I'll get it off him later.'

The twins were both fast asleep and they snored loudly from too much alcohol. Nigel crept into the room and looked on the dressing table.

'Harry!' Nigel nudged him. Harry didn't stir. He pulled back the covers to see the wallet clasped tight in Harry's hands. He tried to pull at it but Harry's grasp was too strong. Oh never mind, he thought, I'll see to it in the morning. He sneaked out of the twins' room and across the landing to the staff bedroom.

Chapter seventeen The Ghost Catalyst

It was dark and cold. A fine veil of frost covered the ground outside. The wind howled through the leafless trees and the sound of the twins snoring rattled through the night. The twins were both still sound asleep suffering from too much alcohol. Suddenly, Harry woke up and sat bolt upright.

'Mum?' he said, and then he covered his mouth with his hand. Winston woke up. 'Mum?' he said incredulously. Then he also put his hands over his mouth.

Stood in the doorway was the ghostly figure of their mother. The ghost spoke.

'Oh take your hands away from your mouths you daft sods, don't you think I know you can speak. I'm your mother! Don't you think I know my own boys? Oh I know how it started. When you were children it was fun to pretend between yourselves wasn't it? Acting like you were daft, playing everybody up and having this secret between the two of you. But then it escalated and you didn't know how to stop doing it did you? I know you haven't been happy for a long time, have you? But what were you supposed to do? Just stand up one day and say "we've been pretending all these years." You were frightened that if you did that, it would upset your Dad and I, weren't you? I don't know! You're both of you a pair of silly sausages. Anyway, Dad and I are gone now. I've come to tell you it's got to stop! You don't really want to spend your life here, being looked after. Do you? I want you to leave tonight while you've got the chance. I know what you really want to do. You should be good at it. I've been watching you all these years and you've had plenty of practice. Bye, my darlings.'

The ghost blew a kiss and then disappeared.

The twins looked at each other then got up, opened their wardrobes and started to get dressed over the top of their pyjamas. Then they took the wallet and the present Mum had bought them and sneaked downstairs. Harry took their birth certificates and passports out of the drawer.

'We might need these,' he said, and they put on their warm winter coats, hats and scarves and ventured out into the night.

It was the most dark and stormy of winter's nights as the twins embarked on a journey that would change the rest of their life. They sat in the bus station. Winston still had the wrapped up birthday present and Harry had the wallet. They had no luggage. A full moon shone through the dark purple clouds that drifted across the night sky, casting dark gloomy shadows. A few stars were visible like diamonds on a black canvas. The wind howled eerily through the trees and Harry and Winston felt more than a bit on edge and a little bit frightened. It began to rain and it lashed against the glass windows of the station. Harry and Winston were glad they made it to the bus station shelter in time; otherwise, they would have been wet through.

'How long is the bus going to be?' asked Winston, shivering.

'I think the first one's half past six in the morning,' said Harry, rubbing his hands together.

'So we've got to wait here all night?'

'That's right.'

'It's cold.'

'I know.'

'Where are we going, anyway?'

'Blackpool.'

'Why Blackpool?'

'I just know. We've got to go to Blackpool. It's where Mum and Dad went for their honeymoon.'

'How much have we got? One thousand pounds?'

'Yes.'

'That's not going to last long, not between the two of us. Especially in Blackpool.'

'We'll be all right. Mum said so.'

They didn't know exactly what they were going to do in Blackpool but they both felt that everything would work out okay. They weren't sure if they had really seen their mother or whether it had been some weird dream, but it felt right to leave the scheme. Eventually, half past six came, their bus arrived and they got on it.

Back at the twins' house, the alarm clock went off. Nigel got out of bed — he had his pyjamas on — and he stretched and yawned. He went along the corridor to the twins' room and opened the door to see they were not there.

'Strange,' he commented to himself. He went downstairs shouting. 'Harry, Winston!'

The twins arrived at the bus station in Blackpool and walked down towards the seafront. The air was fresh, a wind was up and the waves crashed against the sea wall causing sprays of saltwater to lash against the twins' faces. It was still dark. The twins found a bench inside a shelter and they sat down. A man walked past with his dog. It sniffed at the twins' feet as they walked past. Then, an elderly couple walked by; the man had a walking stick and he leaned heavily into as he walked. The twins were surprised to see so many people out and about at this unearthly hour in the morning, especially a cold, dark winter's morning. Harry didn't ever remember being up so early before. They usually got woken up about half past nine. They certainly wouldn't go out anywhere till gone half past ten. The sea air and cold had turned the twins' cheeks a bright crimson colour. Their breath billowed into small white clouds in front of them. Seagulls came and pecked the pavement in front of them. They looked at the twins, heads cocked and through one eye, as though expecting some sort of tasty morsel from them.

'I'm cold and hungry,' said Winston.

'Me too,' said Harry. 'We'll book into a hotel later, as soon as they open.'

'How much will that cost?'

'Don't know. Don't worry; I know we'll be okay.'

'Was that really Mum we saw or some weird shared dream?'

'Dunno.'

They sat and watched the sun come up. They had never seen the sunrise before. They watched as the sun rose in a semi-circle of brilliant orange, disappearing now and again behind the dark clouds that blanketed the sky. Presently, it became lighter as the darkness faded and ascended into the heavens. It started to spit with rain. The twins decided they had better try to find a guesthouse.

Michael was sat at a table across from a woman drinking coffee. The woman was disgruntled and having a moan at Michael.

'So he said if he has to clean, I have to do the garden, but that's not in my job description is it? We can get a gardener in to do the garden,' said the woman, 'housework has to be done; if he can't do it he shouldn't be a support worker. I have to do it. I mean, you should have seen the dust on the television when I came in. It doesn't take much to get a duster out. And he left a dirty cup in the sink. I mean, it doesn't take much to rinse a cup out does it? He took them out to see a band last night you know. Imagine going out, enjoying yourself, and leaving dust everywhere. I don't know how he sleeps at night with the house in such a mess. I couldn't. I wouldn't dream of taking people out when there's cleaning to be done and housework. That's what is called being responsible as an adult.'

'Hmm…' said Michael. He personally thought taking people out for social interaction occasionally was more important than having the house perfect. He wondered if he should get into a row with the women by saying as much.

Michael's mobile phone rang and he answered it. Just on cue, he thought to himself. Good old Iris.

'Hello Iris. An *emergency* in one of the houses you say? Okay, I'm on my way. What? You mean a *real* emergency?'

Michael looked up at the women, wondering if she heard his gaff.

'I mean a *really* important emergency,' He recovered. 'Okay, I'm on my way.' Michael stood up. 'I'm really sorry, I must run.'

Michael pulled up outside the twins' house. A police car was in the driveway. He opened the door with his key and went inside. Nigel was taking to the police. The policeman stood in the front room; a tall brawny man. His uniform hid his well-toned muscular body. He stood with his feet apart, playing with his truncheon. A policewoman sat on the chair taking notes in a small pad.

'I searched the house from top to bottom before calling you,' said Nigel. 'Even inside the wardrobes, under the beds, under the stairs, the garden, the shed. Nothing.'

'You say you saw them both asleep in bed at ten p.m.?' asked the policeman.

'Yes, they were definitely there then!'

'And you heard nothing.'

'I'm afraid not.' Tears started welling in his eyes. 'I feel so responsible, I should have heard something but I was asleep.'

'Come now, it's not your fault,' said Michael, trying to comfort him.

'I feel like it is. I was on duty at the time.'

'Nonsense,' said Michael.

'You were asleep, on duty?' asked the policeman.

'Of course, I was on a sleep-in,' retorted Nigel.

'You don't think they've been kidnapped do you?' Michael suggested.

'Kidnapped?' said the policeman. 'What do you mean kidnapped? Why would anyone want to kidnap them?'

'Well, the twins' family are quite wealthy. They own stables.'

'We can't rule anything out at this stage,' said the policeman. 'We will be distributing photographs to the press and conducting a search of the local area. We have a description of the pyjamas they were wearing. We will be starting the search immediately, considering the vulnerability of the men involved. Time is of the essence, so if you will excuse me.'

'Of course,' said Nigel.

'Forensic will be around later to take fingerprints,' said the policeman. 'Just in case they have been abducted.'

They left, screeching away in their car, sirens sounding.

Winston and Harry were in a hotel room with two double beds, an en suite shower room, a television set, wardrobes, and tea and coffee making facilities.

'Have we to open the present?' asked Winston.

'Yes,' Harry said, getting excited. It was an intriguing parcel.

Winston ripped the wrapping paper off.

'Oh, it's a telescope. Can you put it together?'

'I don't know,' said Harry. 'Has it got instructions?' He started taking the bits out of the box. Winston got on the floor and started examining the pieces with Harry.

'I think I can put this together,' said Winston.

'Good. You do that and I'll go to the shop and get some supplies in.'

Harry left the hotel room and Winston started putting the telescope together.

Shortly, Harry arrived back with two plastic carrier bags.

'I've booked an evening meal at reception,' he said. 'I've got these to last us till then.' He emptied cakes, biscuits, cans of pop, tea, milk, sugar and coffee onto one of the beds from one of the bags.

'Did you get the shower stuff?' asked Winston.

'Yes, it's in the other bag,' said Harry.

'Good, I'm dying for a nice hot shower,' said Winston. He rooted through the bag and took out some shower gel. 'What are we going to do for clean clothes? We didn't bring any.'

'We'll have to manage until we get a job,' said Harry.

'How are we going to get a job?'

'I don't know yet.'

A man was sitting behind the desk of the hotel reception .The news was on the television.

'The Plantington twins went missing on Friday night,' said the newscaster. 'A search of the area is underway. The boys had blue and green striped pyjamas on. Both have severe learning difficulties and police are extremely concerned for their safety. Police and local volunteers have been searching nearby woods and parklands and frogmen have been called in to search the canal.'

A picture of the twins was shown on screen.

Just then, the twins walked past and out of the door.

The hotelier did a double take, looked at the television pictures, then back to the twins.

'Nah, can't possibly be,' he said, flapping his hand. He shook his head and continued watching television.

'Did you hear that on the T.V? Good job you booked us in with false names Harry,' said Winston.

The twins walked along the prom when Harry pointed to a sign that read '*Auditions now being held*'.

'That's it! That's our job! Come on.'

The twins went into the building. There were lots

of people sat around waiting for the auditions. Some of them had come in costume.

'Which parts are we auditioning for?' asked Winston.

'The ugly sisters, of course.'

People got called onto the stage one by one. Harry and Winston listened in as the director kept calling 'next.' They had been given a short script to read. Then it was their turn.

They went on stage and a man gave them a chair and a shoe as props. Winston sat down on the chair and Harry tried to shove the shoe on his foot.

'It's got to fit,' said Harry in a put-on female voice.

'Push harder,' said Winston, also in a high-pitched female voice. 'It'll go on in a minute.'

Winston slid onto the floor with his leg up in the air and Harry continued to try and shove the shoe on his foot.

'Try harder, push harder, it's nearly on,' said Winston.

'It's no use,' said Harry. 'Here, let me have a go — try my foot.'

He held his hand out to Winston to help him up but Winston pulled him to the floor as well. Harry held his foot out and put his toes in the shoe. Winston, still on the floor, grabbed the shoe and tried to push it on Harry's foot. He got onto his knees and put the whole force of his body into shoving the shoe on Harry's foot.

The director was in stitches.

'Stop! Stop!' he said, laughing. 'Perfect. You two are perfect, made for the part. See you here on Thursday night. Five o'clock sharp.'

The twins smiled at each other and left the stage.

When they got out on the street they let out a cry of delight.

'YES!' they both cried. 'We've got a job.'

They were both elated and ran down the pier front, jumping about and shouting. They had both been worried about the money situation and how they were going to gain work, but now they were going to get paid for doing something they loved — acting daft and messing about. They really couldn't believe their luck.

Later in the afternoon, the boys were walking along the beach.

'I can't believe we got a job that easily,' said Winston.

'I knew that was our job,' said Harry. 'That man said we were made for the part, didn't he?'

'Still, I thought it would have been harder. Can we get some new clothes now?'

'No. We won't get paid straight away. That money is for food and board and lodgings. You can get some clothes when we get paid.'

'Shame the Pleasure Beach is shut down,' said Winston. 'Look, that's open.' He pointed to the Ferris wheel. A mist hung half way down it.

'Can we go on it? Please.'

'Okay then, just this once.'

The twins ran over to the wheel excitedly and sat in a carriage. A man approached and took their money. It started up and the boys disappeared into the mist.

'Oh look,' said Harry when they reached the top. 'Blackpool Tower, what a wonderful view.'

'Look down at the mist,' said Winston. 'You almost feel as if you could jump out of the carriage and walk on it.'

They reappeared from out of the mist at the other

side.

'Flipping 'eck, I'm wet through!' said Harry.

'Me too, I'm freezing,' said Winston, rubbing his hands together.

'It's that mist! It's wet! Harry took a handkerchief out of his coat pocket and wiped the damp off his face.

'And it's cold!'

They disappeared again into the mist and then reappeared.

Winston waved at the operator.

'Can you stop this please?' his voice dissipated on the wind.

The operator waved back. The twins disappeared up into the mist and reappeared again. Both of them frantically waved at the operator.

'Stop this thing, we're wet,' they said, their voices melting into the mist.

The operator waved back. 'You're okay. You've got another five minutes yet,' he said as he held his thumbs up.

The twins disappeared and reappeared again. The operator waved again. The twins looked at each other, folded their arms and disappeared once again into the fog.

'Oh flipping 'eck. Whose idea was this? Harry, why didn't you notice it was foggy?'

'Don't blame me.'

'I'm cold.'

'It was *your* idea! Don't blame me.'

Later on, back at the guesthouse, Winston was washing his shirt out in the sink with liquid hand wash in the shower room. He put it on the radiator next to

Harry's. Both of them were in their pyjamas. Harry was sat up in bed. Winston went to look through the telescope, which was set up at the window.

'See anything?' asked Harry.

'Not much, there's too much cloud — also too much glare from all the lights. Funny, Mum leaving us a telescope to see the stars, and now we are both going to be stars.'

'Don't exaggerate, Winston. We're not going to be famous overnight. It's only a small theatre. We probably won't get paid that much either.'

'Still, it's a bit of a coincidence.'

'When we get a clear night, we'll be able to look and see if we can see the rings of Saturn. They say you can see them through a small telescope,' said Harry, yawning. 'Anyway, it's twelve o'clock. I'm going to sleep.'

'Okay, me too.'

Winston climbed into the double bed and switched the light off. Harry drifted off to sleep in the half-light. He started snoring. In his dreams, he was back at the funeral. He saw his brother John handing him the wallet.

'Here you are boys, Dad's smelly old wallet. Dad's smelly old wallet…'

'Awe, isn't that sweet,' said a lady's voice.
Everybody starts laughing

'Dad's smelly old wallet, she left the twins' Dad's smelly old wallet.'

John and his sister were laughing.

'We got the stables, they got Dad's smelly old wallet, Dad's smelly old wallet. He, he, he, he, the twins got Dad's smelly old wallet.'

Harry tossed and turned, his body sweating. He

made moaning noises in his sleep. He saw his mum.

'You can't stay here all your life being looked after. You know what you want to do. Your dad and I are going now. It's up to you now, bye my darlings.' She blew a kiss.

Suddenly, Harry was back as child. He and Winston were playing with the wallet. His dad was there, sat on a winged Chesterfield chair.

'You like that wallet, don't you boys?' said dad. 'It's my favourite wallet. I bought it when your Mum and I were on honeymoon. That's not why it's my favourite though. Here.'

He took the wallet off Harry. He twisted the wallet and flicked it. 'It's got a secret compartment, look.'

Harry woke suddenly and sat up in bed.

'Urrggghh.' He got out of bed and went to get the wallet.

Winston woke up. 'What's wrong?' he said.

Harry turned the wallet upside down and opened it. Nothing happened.

'What's wrong?' repeated Winston.

'It's got a secret compartment,' said Harry. 'I remember Dad saying.'

'Let's look!' said Winston, grabbing for the wallet excitedly.

'No I can do it,' said Harry, pulling away and turning the wallet around and opening it.

'Let me look,' said Winston. 'Here, I bet I can do it.'

They both made a grab for the wallet. The wallet fell open and a bankcard fell onto the floor, wrapped in a piece of paper. Harry picked it up and read the note.

My Dear Boys, if you are reading this, it means I have passed over. Please don't be upset;

I've had a good life. I want you to get on with your lives and be happy. I don't know if you will find this or one of the staff. The card can get you access to a savings account I opened for you both. I know you can use a card Harry — I've seen you in town. I hope you use it to get a better life. If the staff find this, please use the money as best you see fit to help Winston and Harry have an enjoyable life. Take them on holiday or something.

Love you always,

Mum.

P.S I nearly forgot. The pass number is the number of hours I was in labour. Then the number of minutes Winston came after Harry. I know you've heard me tell that tale so often.

The boys looked at each other bemused. 'She's left us some more money,' said Harry. 'I wonder how much.'

The next morning, the twins got up early and set out looking for a cash machine. They found one outside a bank near the bus station. Harry put the bankcard in the machine and keyed in the security code. Twenty-five, thirty.

'So, how much is there?' asked Winston.

'I think there's something wrong with the machine,' said Harry. 'There can't be that much.'

'How much does it say?'

'Half a million pounds.'

'Oh my God, were rich!' He started jumping up and down.

'Calm down,' said Harry. 'It's a mistake. It must be! I didn't know Mum had that much money.'

'Well,' explained Winston 'She did get a share of

the stable's profits and she hardly ever spent anything. She must have invested it.'

'Can we get some clothes now?'

'I suppose so!'

'Yes! Yes! Yes!' Winston ran on the spot, rubbing his hands together.

'Come on then, draw some money out,' said Winston. 'Let's get shopping.'

'Well okay, but it still seems a lot. We'd better be careful in case it's a mistake.'

Harry drew out three hundred pounds and stuffed it in the wallet. They then hit the shops. They really enjoyed being out shopping on their own and trying various clothes on. They bought a pair of black pants each, a couple of shirts and two pairs of jeans each, some underwear, some t-shirts and a new pair of trainers each.

'We need a new suit each, in case we go out at night,' said Winston. 'I bet there will be a party after opening night — we'll need something nice to wear.'

Harry and Winston trawled the shops but everything was black, blue and grey and, well, boring. They tried on suit after suit but nothing seemed quite right. Then Harry saw a florescent yellow suit with matching top hat. It was in the window of a small designer shop.

'There,' he said. 'That's it.'

Winston looked at the price tag. 'It's eight hundred and fifty quid — that's a bit pricey.'

'We can afford it,' said Harry. 'We'll just have to get some more money out.' Harry went into the shop and Winston followed.

'Can I try the suit on in the window?' he said to the shopkeeper. The shopkeeper got the suit out of the window and Harry went into the changing rooms. The suit fitted perfectly, apart from being a bit long in the leg.

'I can take that up for you,' said the shopkeeper.

'What do you think, Winston?' Harry said, moving from side to side, posing and looking in the mirror.

'It's perfect,' said Winston. 'We'll take two.'

'Actually, it's supposed to be a one-off,' said the shopkeeper. 'I suppose I could make another one exactly the same, but it would take a few weeks and I'd need a deposit.'

'Do it!' said Harry and Winston in unison. They paid what money they had left as deposit then, exhausted from all the shopping, they went and got a coffee.

Chapter Eighteen The Ugly Sisters

Julie was at home on sick leave; she hadn't slept properly since the twins' disappearance and was suffering from nervous exhaustion. She decided to ring Calder Fields Place to see if there was any news. Nigel picked up the phone.

'Have you heard anything Nigel?' asked Julie.

'Nothing helpful,' said Nigel. 'You wouldn't believe it Julie; some horrible prankster rang the police to say they had seen the twins in a hotel in Blackpool.'

'How do they know it's a hoax?'

'This person said it was definitely the men he'd seen on the news, but they were wearing not pyjama's but, get this, yellow florescent suits with matching hats. According to this prankster, they were drinking margaritas and got up on the karaoke and sang *New York, New York*. Apparently, he got quite aggressive when the police suggested it couldn't be them. He said they looked just like the guys on the T.V. and he was talking to them. He said they were staying at Betty's Boarding House.'

'So did the police check it then?' asked Julie.

'Julie, how could that be the boys?' said Nigel. 'Come on love, I know you miss them but it was obviously just some nasty prankster. Quite frankly, I hope they throw the book at him. No! I hate to say this Julie but I think the possibility of the boys still being alive is getting slimmer by the minute. So when are you coming back to work? They're very short staffed in the other houses.'

'I don't think I will be coming back, actually.'

'Oh come on Julie!' Nigel pleaded. 'We've all been upset and affected by this, but, well, it's one of those things. Nasty things happen sometimes. You've just got to get on with life. You realise, if the twins don't turn up soon, we'll be getting new people at Calder Fields Place.'

'I know Nigel, that's why I don't want to come back. It would be just awful working in the twins' house with someone else, not knowing what happened to them both. I think it's time I turned my hand to something different. I think as soon as I'm fit back for work I'm going to look for another job.'

'Oh come on now Julie, this has affected us all. We're short staffed on the scheme as it is. We can't afford to lose good staff like you.'

'I'm afraid I've made up my mind Nigel. I'm leaving.'

'Oh well, if I can't change your mind, good luck then! Bye for now.'

'Bye Nigel.'

Julie put the phone down.

Hmm... Betty's Boarding House, she thought to

herself. She wasn't as convinced as Nigel that it was a hoax. She decided to go and check it out, for her own peace of mind.

Julie turned up at Betty's Boarding House with a small suitcase.

The reception desk was small, with a guest book and telephone. Betty herself was manning the front desk.

'Have you got a room for the night?'

'I think we have some vacancies, let's look. Ah, yes, room number twelve.' Betty handed Julie a key. 'There you are, my love. Up two flights of stairs; it's on your left. There's a meter on the wall for the hot water for the shower. Breakfast is between eight and nine o'clock.'

'Thank you,' said Julie. She made her way up the stairs with her suitcase.

The desk phone rang and Betty answered it.

'Hello, Betty's Boarding House.'

'Hello, can I book in for Christmas Eve?' said the voice on the other end of the phone.

'I'm afraid we're fully booked over Christmas.'

'How about New Year's Eve then?' said the voice.

'New Year is a two-night stay minimum. I'm sorry about that love; I've been booked up for months now. You'd be lucky to get in any of the boarding houses. Some of the bigger hotels may have vacancies. Sorry I couldn't help my love. Bye.'

The twins came down the stairs. They had on black pants, white shirts and silver jackets.

'How's it going my loves?' Betty asked. 'You booked up?'

'Almost full house for the rest of the week,' replied Harry.

'Well, break a leg then,' said Betty.

'Pardon?' Harry asked, confused. Break a leg? What did she want him to break a leg for, had she found out about them? He had never heard the expression before. Why would the landlady want him to break one of his legs? Was she some kind of psychopath? He gave her a funny look.

'Come on,' said Winston, breaking into Harry's thoughts. 'We don't want to be late.'

He took Harry's arm and led him out of the boarding house. Harry still looked back over his shoulder at Betty with a look of horror on his face.

'Why does she want us to break a leg Winston? Does she know who we are?'

'I don't know,' replied Winston. 'I was thinking the same thing.'

They had a brief discussion about what they would do if the police turned up, and then carried on their way.

Upstairs, Julie was glancing out of the window.

'Oh my! It's them; it's the twins.'

She ran out of the room, downstairs and out of the boarding house onto the street. The street was quite crowded. People walking up and down with kiss me quick hats on with various flashing luminous necklaces and other objects. People had large cuddly toys under their arms, sharks and teddy bears. A nun flew past on a skateboard. At least it looked like a nun. A group of transvestites tottered about on their higher than high heals, handbags waving. People queued at the tram station. The traffic was bumper-to-bumper — coming in to see the illuminations — and crawled past, horns blaring. A horse and carriage trotted past. The air smelt of sea salt, hot doughnuts and fish and chips. Seagulls fought and screeched over scavenged scraps people had thrown on the floor. The cold wind went straight through her clothes, chilled her to the bone and whistled in her ear. The sound of the sea's crashing waves echoed in her ears. Julie spotted the twins in the distance and made after them, dodging the crowd. She caught up behind them but said nothing, walking silently a few feet behind them. The twins turned down a back street and into the side door of a small theatre. Julie watched, then walked round to the front to see a sign that read:

Cinderella Starring Claudette Fishmonger (local Brittany Spears tribute artist) Introducing: The Stargazey Twins — Aries and Pluto — as the two ugly sisters.

Julie walked into the box office.

'Excuse me, what time does the performance start?'

'Six-thirty p.m.,' replied the lady sat in the box office.

'Hmm…' said Julie. 'It's five now. You haven't by any chance got any tickets left?'

The box office lady started to type on her computer.

'How many is it for?'

'Just one.'

'You're in luck — we have five seats left. I'm afraid they're right at the back.'

'That's fine.'

Julie purchased the ticket and then went to get some tea; she sat on a pier bench eating fish and chips out of a bag. It was very windy and the tide was coming in, lashing against the pier wall. Julie finished her chips, which were wrapped in newspaper, and then she scrunched the paper up. Just then, she spotted the twins' faces on the newspaper. She un-scrunched the newspaper and straightened it. The twins' picture was on the page and they were dressed in football wear. Julie read:

Hat trick for charity twins. The annual charity football match (proceeds to clinical research of genetic conditions) was held last week on Blackpool beach. The Stargazey twins scored one goal each. They had sponsored themselves £500 for each goal they scored, prompting people to say it was a blatant attempt to bribe the goalkeeper to dive the other way. Still, they were triumphant as they handed over the £1000 cheque. The Event made £2500 altogether. The Stargazey twins are currently in pantomime, starring as the ugly sisters.

'Wow,' thought Julie.

Julie walked back down the promenade and joined the queue for the theatre. She sat at the back of the theatre in semi darkness. The lights came on the stage; the curtains opened and the twins came on stage.

'Hello boys and girls!'

'Hello,' chanted the audience.

'Has anybody seen that lazy Cinderella?' asked Harry.

'Cinderella's not lazy,' chirped a little boy on the front row.

'Who said that?' asked Harry, twisting his head round from one side to the other.

'Oh look, she's left us something to eat,' said Winston, going towards a big pan on a stove. He scooped some liquid up with a ladle.

'Orrghhh, tastes like smelly old socks!'

Harry went over and pulled a dripping sock out of the pan. '*It is* smelly old socks, you fool! She's been boiling the laundry.'

Chinks of laughter came from the audience.

Harry went stomping off but tripped over a mop and bucket, ending on his bottom with his legs flapping in the air.

'That silly girl, imagine leaving that there. Help me up will you?'

Winston tried to pull him up but both of them ended up on the floor.

'This is Cinderella's fault. Just wait till we get hold of her.'

The audience laughed. Julie smiled and shook her head. Finally, the twins made it to their feet.

'We're going to look for Cinderella,' said Harry. 'Now, if you see her shout me won't you?'

'No way! Booooooo' shouted a little boy.

Harry flapped his hand in mock disgust at the boy and both of them exited off stage.

Julie couldn't believe what she was seeing. Everybody had been worrying themselves sick over the twins and here they were, playing two ugly sisters in pantomime. Getting their name in the paper over their charity work. Julie decided not to say anything; after all, nobody on the scheme would believe it was the same men. She had seen them now, she knew they where okay. She decided to sneak out of the performance early and book out of Betty's before the twins got back. She didn't want to spoil this new life they seemed to have made for themselves.

Also in the theatre was an agent. He hadn't come out talent scouting; he'd just brought his kids to the pantomime. However, he liked the twins — he felt they had talent. He could also think of a few jobs that were looking out for twins. He thought he would approach them about going on his books after the performance was over.

Chapter Eighteen The Passion

Spring was in the air. As always, it was time for out with the old, in with the new. Birds built their nests ready for the egg laying season in the trees that grew along Calder Fields Place. Tulips and daffodils were out in full bloom in the neighbourhood gardens.

Michael rang the doorbell of the twins' old house and Nigel answered the door. He had in his hand a paintbrush loaded with pink paint, which was also in his hair.

'Come in,' said Nigel and both walked through into the living room.

'So, how did your morning with the new service user go?' asked Michael.

'Oh quite well,' replied Nigel. 'She's looking forward to moving in. She opted out of new wallpaper for her bedroom and decided she would like the room painted this lovely shade of flamingo pink. What do you think?' He held out the paintbrush.

'Hmm… Ah well, it's her room,' said Michael.

'If you'll excuse me,' said Nigel. 'I'll just go and put this in a plastic bag, before it dries out. Would you like a coffee?"

'Yes please!'

Michael got up, took the T.V. remote control off the shelf and turned on the news. 'Oh that's terrible! Have you seen this? There's been a terrible earthquake on one of the Greek islands.'

Nigel shouted back from kitchen 'You are joking me?'

'No, some of the hotels have been flattened, casualties, a few fatalities.'

Nigel came back into the room with two coffees

'What about Mary who supports James?' asked Nigel. 'She's gone to Greece for her holidays, hasn't she?'

'Hmm, I think she's in Athens though,' said Nigel.

'Thank God.'

Michael turned his back to the television. 'So everything went okay then?'

'Yes,' said Nigel. 'She should be moving in at the end of the week. I must admit, it feels funny moving somebody else in. I know it's over six months since they disappeared — the twins — but it feels really horrible painting their room, like I'm painting over them or something.'

'Yes, that was a real tragedy,' said Michael, drinking his coffee. 'I wonder what happened to them?'

Nigel spluttered on his coffee and pointed to the television.

'What?' said Michael.

The twins were on the television screen, dancing about in bright red dishevelled wigs and thick glasses. A tuneful voice over sang: 'Two times the oats, two times the fruit, and two times the nuts in Kaizer's Breakfast Nutty Fruit Bar.'

'It's the twins! Look!' said Nigel.

'No!' said Michael, glancing at the television. Granted, the blokes on television did resemble the twins, but how could it possibly be them? The twins had severe learning difficulties.

'Look!' insisted Nigel. 'If you take away the red wigs, the glasses. LOOK!'

'Nigel, you've been under strain lately. I think

your mind is playing tricks on you. You're missing the twins, and then you see two actors on T.V., dressed in the same clothes like the twins used to do who, I must admit, resemble the twins — and well. You start seeing things that aren't there. It couldn't possibly be the twins, now could it?'

'No! I suppose not. They did bear a resemblance though. Amazing! Two of them as well.'

'We do have a counselling service you know.'

'I don't need counselling.'

'Well, I have been wondering. I mean, it was you on shift when they disappeared into thin air. It's possible you're harbouring a guilt complex. I mean, not that it was your fault or anything.'

Nigel became quite agitated.

'WHAT? NO! No counsellors, I'm fine.'

'There's no shame in seeking help, you know.'

'For the last time, no counsellors, absolutely not, I'm fine.'

'But…'

'NO! NO! NO!…….No!'

'Okay,' said Michael. 'If you're sure. Well, I better get going.' He left the house, climbed into his baby blue Rover and drove back to the office.

Michael walked into the office. Iris was filing her nails. She stood up to greet Michael.

'You'll never guess what? Julie's rang — she's coming back next week.'

'Great, wonderful,' said Michael. He really was pleased — it was hard work getting the right staff. In fact, he felt like hugging Iris for being the bearer of good news. He thought about the earthquake and the twins disappearing without trace. Lives to short for procrastination, he thought, seize the day and all that. He grabbed Iris and took her in his arms. He half expected a slap but it wasn't forthcoming. Instead, electricity cackled between them, sending bolts of shivers down their bodies. Seize the day, thought Michael. He kissed her — just a peck on the lips at first to see if she'd object. She didn't. In fact, she practically melted on the spot. Michael kissed her again, this time pushing his tongue into her mouth. Iris felt her stomach flip over and an electric jolt started in her stomach, lowering to her pelvis. She felt moistness between her legs. She responded to his advances, kissing him back, and they pressed heavily against each other — each of them feeling electricity and heat stirring within their groins. A warm glow encased them as they kissed, tasting each other's sweetness. They were entwined in passion's sweet embrace and locked together, breathing heavily as they explored each other's tongues; holding each other tight.

Iris could feel Michael's hardness being pushed against her groin, making her wet. She longed for him, for his body. They were both hard and horny. Michael grabbed her legs, hitching up her skirt, and lifted her up so she straddled him. Then he walked forwards with her legs around him and laid her on the desk, sending the In/Out tray and her handbag flying. He pulled down her tights and knickers and pulled down his pants. Iris groaned as he pushed his hot hard manhood inside her. Her body was on fire and she could feel Michael's heat rising inside her. He undid her high heals that were now by his shoulders and then pulled them off and pulled her underwear off over her feet. He suckled on her toes, sending shock waves down Iris's body that ended in her brain. Explosions were going off in her head. Then he leaned over to kiss her mouth again, pushing his tongue back inside hers. Their bodies became one. Heated and sweaty, they pushed and ground against each other. Tongues entwined, they puffed and grunted; their hearts racing with the love they felt between them and the excitement of the possibility of getting caught. He undid her blouse and gently suckled on one of her nipples. Iris gasped quietly, running her fingers through Michael's hair. Hungry for each other's love, they grabbed and stroked each other's bodies; their skin tingling and electrified with the feel of each other's touch. Iris put her hands up inside his shirt and dug her nails into Michael's back. Michael thought of objecting — his wife might see the scratches — but he was too carried away and didn't want to spoil the moment. He'd think of some excuse later. Iris felt like crying — she was so overcome with emotion. She couldn't believe this was finally happening after all these years of her secretly loving him. She felt like her chest was going to explode with the weight of her heart. Michael began to thrust deeper and faster, deeper and faster. A fire raged in his groin that had spread upwards into his belly. He couldn't believe he was actually making love to Iris and she was letting him. A bead of perspiration dropped of his forehead and landed on Iris's lip. She tasted his saltiness. Suddenly, Michael let out a cry as he came to orgasm. Iris shuddered as she climaxed at the same moment, feeling his manhood trembling inside of her. Both of their bodies quivered and shuddered. A whole host of angels started singing in their ears as Michael collapsed on top of her. Iris stroked his hair and kissed his cheek.

'I love you,' said Iris.

'I love you too,' said Michael.

Both of them, happy but slightly embarrassed as this was their first encounter, got up and dressed hurriedly. Iris buttoned her blouse up on the wrong buttons, her face was red and puffed and her usually neat hair was untidy. Michael pulled his trousers up and tucked his shirt in. He too was red-faced, his spikes had been flattened and he had lipstick all around his mouth.

'Come here,' said Iris. She pulled a tissue off the office desk and wiped the lipstick from his face.

'Thanks,' said Michael.

Iris put the In /Out tray back on the desk. Michael went into his office.

'Call me if you need me,' he said over his shoulder.

'Yes, Mr Fenchurch,' said Iris, as she looked in a vanity mirror to tidy her hair and retouch her makeup. Her head was spinning. Where does it go from here? she thought. Was that just a one-off or the beginning of a beautiful relationship? She felt slightly sick. She couldn't bear it seeing Michael every day if that was it. She hoped it would happen again. Michael was feeling the same way. He thought of inviting her away for the weekend. He was okay — he could tell his wife there was a staff shortage in one of the houses — but what could Iris tell her husband? He would have to think of something. He wanted to spend some time with her away from work. He had an idea of being in a hotel bedroom, watching television and curled up with a bottle of wine or even champagne. He might even take her out to a show and certainly for a nice meal somewhere. She could say she had to go on a course. Yes — he'd run it by her later.

Chapter Nineteen, Stargazing

The air hung heavy with cigarette smoke that caught in the lights of the discothèque. Rave music blared away and people danced on the dance floor, waving their arms in the air. Harry and Winston leaned on the bar. They were in London. Their agent had advised them there was more work in London than up north and had got them sorted out with a hotel room. They had got paid handsomely for the advert they had done on television and had a comedy play lined up as well as work as extras in a film that BBC1 was producing. The twins couldn't be happier. They were getting paid for doing what they liked doing — pretending — and they found they had an amazing ability to memorise lines, which helped no end in their acting career. They enjoyed living out of hotel rooms. They had no bills to pay. They had their meals cooked. They'd even been eating out in posh restaurants. For once in their life, they could do as they pleased. No staff telling them what to do. They wore their favourite yellow suits and drank cocktails. Two young ladies walked up to the bar.

'Would you like a drink, ladies?' offered Winston.

'No thanks,' said the girls.

Winston looked at Harry and they both sighed. They weren't having much luck with the ladies; that was their only gripe with their situation. They didn't know why —they both thought they looked handsome in their yellow suits with matching hats.

'Want to dance?' said Harry.

'Okay,' said Winston.

They got up on the dance floor and started

flailing their limbs about wildly to the music. Neither of them had given much of a thought to Julie or the scheme, or John and Sarah back at the stables. They were too busy with their new life to give much thought to the past. Things had really taken off in a way that neither of them expected. They thought about their mum often. They liked to think she was looking down on them and approving of their new life. She'd always said they'd do something to make them proud one day and now here they were in London on the verge of stardom.

'I'm getting tired of the smoky atmosphere,' said Harry. 'Have we to go back to the hotel?'

'Okay,' said Winston.

They walked, slightly staggering from the alcohol, into the street. The smell of kebab lured them into Zorba's for a midnight feast. They both ordered shish kebab with garlic sauce and sat down on a bench to eat it. The streets were quiet, save for the odd drunk staggering about. They finished their kebabs and then made their way back to the hotel. The bar was still open so they decided to have one more drink before heading off to bed. They ordered two margaritas. Two ladies sat up taking at a table. They were quite young — in their late twenties — and wore tight trousers with loose blouses. They looked like sisters. Both of them had brown eyes and long, flowing brown hair.

'Look,' said the elder one, nudging her sister and giggling. 'It's the blokes off that advert.'

'That's right,' said Harry. 'Do you want our autograph?'

'No thanks,' said the younger one, still giggling.

'Would you like a drink?' said Winston.

'Yes please, we'll have a gin and tonic each if you don't mind,' said the older one.

Winston ordered two gin and tonics at the bar and then they both went over with the drinks and sat with the girls at the table.

'So what are your names?' asked Winston.

'I'm Tanya,' the older one replied, 'and this is Sonya, my sister. And your names?'

'I'm Pluto and this is Aries,' said Harry.

'Those are funny names,' said Sonya.

'Actually, those are our stage names,' said Winston, shuffling in his chair uncomfortably. It was the first time they had got into conversation with some girls and he could feel his face flushing red. 'Our real names are Winston and Harry. I'm Winston and this is Harry.'

'I think I prefer Pluto and Aries,' said Sonya. 'What made you pick those names?'

'We like looking at the stars,' said Harry. 'Pluto is a planet and Aries is a constellation.'

'Oh, I'm into horoscopes,' said Tanya. 'What's your star sign?'

'Libra,' said Harry. 'We're both Libra — were twins.'

'You'd never had guessed,' said Tanya.

'Why? Do you not think we look like each other?' asked Winston.

'I was joking,' said Tanya, taking a cigarette out of her purse. 'I can't tell you apart to be honest.'

'That's a bad habit,' said Harry, playing with his glass. 'It's bad for your health.'

'I know,' replied Tanya, giving one to her sister. 'I keep meaning to give up. So, you're Librans? That means you're even-tempered and well-balanced.'

'I wouldn't say we're well balanced,' said Winston. 'We're actors — artistic temperament and all that. What do you girls do?'

'I'm a nurse,' said Tanya. 'I work in an old people's home. My sister works in telesales — she sells car insurance.'

'Oh, we don't have a car. We can't drive,' said Harry. 'That must be interesting being a nurse?'

'I suppose so. I work with people with Alzheimer's, so it's hard work. The poor old dears keep shouting for their tea when they've just eaten. They forget they've just being fed and it's a dirty job; a lot of them are incontinent and some of them need washing and dressing and feeding. It keeps me fit,' she said, puffing on her cigarette.

'I'm surprised at you a nurse smoking,' said Winston.

'I know. I've tried to give up but it's hard. I've tried everything — patches, nicotine tablets — I even tried hypnotism, but none of it helped.'

Tanya looked Harry and Winston up and down. They certainly were handsome with their brawny broad shoulders, blue eyes and short blonde hair. Their dress sense left something to be desired, but that could be worked on. The good thing was that she and her sister wouldn't have to fight over them. They'd get one each.

'What's your star sign?' asked Winston.

'I'm Aries and my sister is Pisces,' said Tanya.

Sonya stayed quiet and drank her gin and tonic. She was quite drunk and a sense of unreality was setting in as the room began to spin.

'I know,' said Harry. 'Why don't you come up to our room and we can show you our telescope? It's a full moon tonight — you can look at all the craters.'

'Pardon?' Tanya had heard some chat up lines before, but this one took the biscuit.

'Telescope,' said Harry. 'We've got a telescope in

our room. You could come and look at the moon's craters and you can look at Venus as well if you like.'

'Okay,' said Tanya.

She was rather drunk, her inhabitations were down and she liked the twins. She knew if she liked them, her sister would too — they always liked the same blokes.

'I'll get some wine to take up with us,' said Winston. He went to the bar and ordered two bottles of wine and four glasses. He needed more sedative on account of his nerves. He couldn't believe it; two beautiful girls were coming back to their room with them. 'Here Harry, help me carry these.'

Harry took a bottle of wine off him and two glasses and led the way upstairs to their hotel room. Winston followed with the girls trailing behind. Sonya leant heavily on the stair rail on the way up, staggering slightly.

'Where are you two staying?' asked Harry.

'Here of course,' said a drunken Sonya. 'We're here for the week.'

They reached the twins' room and went inside. Harry and Winston put the wine and the glasses down and poured it out.

'Here, look,' said Winston. 'I've directed it towards the moon. You can see the craters.'

Tanya looked through the telescope.

'Oh yes. It's amazing how much detail you can see through a small telescope like this.'

'Let's have a look,' said Sonya, staggering over to the telescope. 'Oh yes, it's amazing isn't it?'

The girls sat down on Harry's double bed and the twins sat down on Winston's. The twins were nervous — they had never been alone with two girls before and they didn't know what to do or say. They sat staring at each other, drinking the wine. The girls wished the twins would make a move on them or say something or do something. They couldn't think of anything to say either. Eventually, Winston spoke.

'Would you like to come out for a meal with us tomorrow night — our treat?'

'Yes,' said Tanya. 'Is that all right with you Sonya?'

'Yes I'd love to,' said Sonya.

'We'll meet you in the hotel bar about seven,' suggested Harry.

'Yes fine,' agreed Tanya. Everything went quite again and they sat there looking at each other uncomfortably. 'Well, we'll be going back to our rooms then. Are you coming Sonya?'

Sonya grunted and stood up off the bed and the girls left. They hovered about the door for a few seconds, as if expecting a kiss or something, but none was forthcoming so they left.

'I can't believe it,' said Harry. 'We've got a date — a first date. Do you think they'll turn up?'

'I can't see why not,' replied Winston. 'They said they would come. Where do you think we should take them?'

'I thought that little Italian restaurant round the corner.' Harry was ecstatic; he could hardly contain his excitement. 'What do you think we should wear?'

'I think we should go shopping tomorrow and get something new for our first date,' suggested Winston.

'Okay,' said Harry.

The twins got undressed and got in bed. They both had the girls filling their thoughts.

'Do you think we should try to kiss them

tomorrow, or do you think they'll go mad and slap us?' asked Winston.

'I don't know,' said Harry. 'We've never kissed a girl before. What if we don't do it properly?'

'I'm really nervous,' said Winston. 'We'll have to see what happens. I'm scared to try and kiss one of them in case they slap us. Anyway, which one are you having?'

'I like Tanya,' said Harry. 'You can have Sonya.'

'Okay, I like Sonya anyway — she's nice and quiet.'

The twins thought of their mum and how proud she'd be. First, they left the scheme to cope on their own. Then they got jobs acting and now they were going on a first date with two lovely ladies. They went to sleep dreaming of the girls, of kissing them, of making love to them. It was all down to them if they could pluck up the courage to make a move. Then, next week, rehearsals for the play would start and they would be doing what they loved doing best — acting daft. The twins couldn't be happier.

Chapter Twenty Suspects

The twins awoke with a start. A loud hammering on the door had interrupted their blissful, dreamful sleep. Dreams full of the girls and sex and romance. Dreams of engagement and marriage and a big house full of children.

'Who's this?' said Harry, sitting up and rubbing his eyes.

'You don't think it's the girls, do you?' asked Winston excitedly. 'Maybe they can't wait until tonight to see us again. I'll get it.' He jumped out of bed and ran to the door, throwing it open.

Stood in the doorway was a police constable. 'You're both wanted for questioning,' he said. 'Come with us.'

The twins looked at each other, horrified.

The ride to the police station was not a comfortable one. They had been handcuffed and locked in the back of the van. It was terribly claustrophobic and they both felt like screaming.

When they got to the police station, they where stripped of their jewelry and the belts off their trousers, and thrown into separate police cells.

Winston lay on the blue mattress on the floor of the police cell. He was frightened. Not only of the situation he was in with the police, but the fact this was the first time he had been separated from his twin brother. He knew Harry would feel the same way. The grate in the door opened.

'Coffee,' said a voice. A policewomen offered him a coffee through the grate. What was this about? he thought.

Harry was in the interview room. He looked nervously at the tape recorder. A policeman and a lawyer came in and the policeman read him his rights.

'What have you done with the Plantington twins?' asked the officer. 'And who are you? You've been drawing money out of their account.'

'We *are* the Plantington twins. I'm Harry,' he protested.

'You've had plastic surgery to look like them or something. The Plantington twins had severe learning difficulties.'

'No, we've been pretending all these years. I can assure you I'm Harry Plantington.'

'You expect me to believe you were pretending to have learning difficulties?'

'Yes, since we were children. It was when Sarah was born. Mum wasn't paying us as much attention anymore so we decided not to speak to her or anybody and we only spoke to each other. Look, I'm telling you the truth.'

'I'm arresting you on suspicion of murder and embezzlement, whoever you are,' said the police officer. 'This has been some elaborate plan to gain access to the twins' money.'

'Wait,' said Harry. 'There's Julie, Julia Summerfield off the scheme we lived on. She knew we were just pretending.'

'Or she could be your accomplice,' suggested the police officer. 'Did this Julia Summerfield give you keys to the house so you could break in and kidnap the Plantington twins? I've been thinking there must have been somebody on the inside.'

'But we *are* the Plantington twins,' said Harry. 'Look, do a D.N.A test or something if you don't believe us.'

'Oh, we intend to — don't worry. We want to know who you really are,' said the constable.

They took Harry back to his cell and interviewed Winston.

Both of their hearts thumped inside their chests. Life had been going so well and now it looked like they could go to prison for the rest of their natural life. They finished speaking to Winston and threw him back in the cell.

They were in prison for three days; fed meals out of little plastic trays. Winston and Harry hated being apart from each other. Plus, they were bored as hell. Harry saw some writing on the wall: C.C.T.V cameras in operation, it said. He started singing and dancing to the camera 'Two times the fruit, two times the nuts. In Kaizer's Fruity Nut Bars. Then the policeman came in. 'Stop messing about,' he said. 'There's someone to see you.'

'Who?' asked Harry.

'John, the twins' brother.'

He led him into a room where Winston was already sat. Harry went and sat down next to him.

Then John came in.

'Hello John!' said Harry and Winston in unison.

' Well, it looks like them but it can't be. Harry and Winston can't speak.'

'Yes we can. We just didn't want to,' said Winston.

'It can't possibly be them officer, my brothers have severe learning difficulties,' explained John. 'Obviously, whoever they are they're in cahoots with that Julie off the scheme. They've obviously had this planned for ages. Mother must have let it slip to Julie that she was leaving the twins a lot of money. They've obviously just been waiting for Mum to die to set their plans into action.' He stared hard at the twins. 'Who are you and what have you done with our brothers?'

'It's not fair, is it John?' said Harry.

'Pardon?' said John.

'That's what you used to say when we did anything naughty — it's not fair. Remember when we poured shampoo over your record collection and we used to rip yours and Sarah's books up? Then there was the time we wound wool around the chair legs and you got the blame for it.'

'Look, we know Julie's your accomplice. She could have got this information out of Mother when she visited the twins. The police have Julie as well. The game's up.'

'Oh my God, you've arrested Julie,' said Winston.

'She's just helping with enquiries at this stage,' said the policeman.

Just then, another officer came to the door.

'Can I have a word?' he said to the first policeman. He pulled him to one side and whispered in his ear.

'Well, who would have believed it?' said the first officer. 'Looks like you're both free to go.

'What?' said John. 'You're just going to let these impostors go?'

'That's the thing,' said the police officer. 'The D.N.A results have come back. It would appear these two *are* your brothers after all.'

John's legs started to wobble and he made for the chair and sat down.

'Mum used to say you were all there with your

cough drops — you were just winding us up,' commented John.

'She was an intelligent women Mum, wasn't she?' said Harry.

John's fist clenched in front of his face. He jumped up to fly at the twins and punch them both in the face, but he remembered where he was just in time. He didn't want to get done for G.B.H.

'You made our lives hell when we were little. Me and Sarah,' he shouted instead of hitting them. 'I'm going to get a lawyer on you. I don't see why you and that snivelling little vet Rod Smith should get all her money. None of you did anything for her. Me and Sarah looked after her for all of these years.'

'You got the stables,' said Winston. 'Anyway, I'm sure she was in sound mind when she wrote the will.'

'Yes,' said Harry. 'I don't think you've got a leg to stand on to be honest.'

'Oh, I'll get you back somehow for spoiling my childhood, you bastards,' said John, making for the door.

Harry and Winston thought they should wait for John to leave before they went back to the hotel. They got a taxi back to the hotel.

'Well, that's it isn't it?' said Winston. 'John and Sarah know all about us now.'

When they got back to the hotel, Harry asked the hotelier about the girls they were supposed to be taking out for dinner.

'They've gone home,' said the hotelier. 'They where awfully upset you both stood them up.'

'Did they leave a forwarding address?' asked Harry, hopefully.

'I'm afraid I can't give out that sort of

information,' said the hotelier.

Harry and Winston went back to their room, feeling really depressed.

A week later, Harry and Winston were on set for the film they were shooting. They were having a rest and a coffee between breaks.

'Have you seen this?' said the tea boy, handing Winston a paper. Winston choked on his coffee.

'Oh my God,' he said.

'What does it say?' said Harry.

'How the Stargazy twins ruined my childhood, by brother John.'

'Let's have a look,' said Harry. 'Oh my God, it's on the front page and centre spread.'

'He said he was going to get his own back, didn't he?' said Winston, blowing his nose with a tissue.

'They say no publicity is bad publicity,' said the tea boy.

Just then, Harry's mobile phone rang.

'Hello,' said their agent on the other end of the phone. 'I've had Parkinson's team on the phone — they want to know if you'll go on his show. They're after a frank interview about your childhood.'

'It's our agent,' said Harry to Winston. 'Do we want to go on the Parkinson show to do a frank interview about our childhood?'

'I suppose so,' said Winston. 'I can't see any harm in it.'

'Yes,' said Harry down the phone. 'We'll do it.'

'Told you,' said the tea boy, laughing. 'There's no such thing as bad publicity when you're an actor.'

'That's given me an idea,' said Winston. 'Why don't we write our autobiography?'

‘I’d have no idea how to start writing a book.’

‘We'll need a computer,’ said Winston, ‘like the staff bought for us on the scheme.’

‘How are we going to carry a computer round with us all over the place?’ asked Harry. ‘Don’t be daft.’

‘You could get a laptop,’ said the tea boy.

‘What’s a laptop?’ asked Winston.

‘It’s like a small computer that fits on your lap. You can get on the internet with them and everything.’

‘What’s the internet?’ said Harry and Winston in unison.

‘Oh my God, where have you two been?’ asked the tea boy in amazement. He couldn’t believe there was anybody who didn’t know what the internet was. He racked his brains trying to think how to describe what the internet was. ‘It’s like an international community where you can share information and talk to people on line.’

'What, like girls?' asked Harry excitedly.

'Yes, they have loads of dating agencies on line.’

‘What’s a dating agency?’ asked Winston.

‘Are you two for real?’ laughed the tea boy. ‘You don’t know what a dating agency is? Well, you pay a fee and they match you up with like-minded women. You can just chat to them or if you like them you can ask them out on a date.’

Harry and Winston both started rubbing their hands together.

‘Mmmmm,’ they both said.

‘Where can we get one of these intertops?’ asked Winston.

‘Internet laptops! Any computer shop or electrical appliances outlet. Comet will still be open tonight when you’ve finished filming. It’s just round the corner on that big industrial estate near the roundabout,' he said helpfully.

'Thanks,' said Harry.

They couldn't wait until filming was over so they could go and buy one.

Soon, five o'clock came. Going home time. They almost ran down the road to the industrial estate. They looked around the shop and found the laptops. A sales assistant came over.

'Can I help you?' he asked.

'Yes, we want to buy a laptop.'

'Well, we have a selection to choose from,' said the sales assistant. 'What did you want it for?'

'Well, we want to go on the internet,' said Harry.

'And write a book,' said Winston.

'Well, any of these will do the job,' said the assistant.

'We'll have that one,' said Winston, pointing to a Compaq.

'You'll need to buy an AOL Internet package plus a firewall,' said the assistant.

'What's a firewall?' asked Winston.

'It's to stop people sending you programs that might damage your computer. Computer viruses and bugs.'

'Well okay,' said Harry. 'We'd better have one of them. Hey, Winston, how many girls do you think we'll meet on these dating agency things.'

'If you're going on the dating sights, you'll probably need to post a picture of yourselves. Would you like a digital camera?' asked the salesman.

'Yes okay,' said Winston.

'How about a digital movie cam as well? Then you can talk to the girls live and see them at the same time.'

'What do you mean?' asked Winston. 'Like the communication devices on *Star Trek* where they can see each other talking?'

'Yes exactly,' said the salesman.

'We'll take one,' said Harry.

'Right,' said the salesman. 'I'll just get your laptop from downstairs. You have to run these disks from each box in your CDRom drive and you're away. Just follow the instructions — it's dead easy. How are you going to pay?'

'Cash card,' said Harry, getting his card out of his pocket.

'You don't need finance?' asked the salesman. 'I can get you on a three-year credit plan.'

'What's a credit-plan?' asked Harry, looking at him quizzically.

'Oh never mind,' said the salesperson. 'Paying by card will be fine.'

The twins purchased their new stuff and Harry rang for a taxi on his mobile phone to take them back to the hotel.

Once back at the room, they unpacked all the stuff and read the instruction manuals.

'It says you need a phone line to get on the internet,' said Winston. 'We haven't got a phone line.'

'Oh dear,' said Harry.

'Well, we can start on our autobiography can't we?' said Winston.

'Where can we start?' asked Harry.

'At the beginning,' said Winston, and he began to type.

Our mother Dora was in labour with us for

twenty-five hours. Harry came first, then myself half an hour later. We shared the womb together. That was the start of an inseparable relationship that would last the rest of our lives.

Just then, Harry's mobile went off. It was their agent.

'Listen darlings, the phone's been going mad,' the agent began. 'I think I've got the perfect job for you. The starring role in a movie set in Manchester. It's a true story about a pair of twins. They're both very difficult — as you where yourselves growing up. Anyway, their mother decides to keep one at home and put the other in an institution. When Christopher grows up, he tries to find his twin brother. He meets up with him and they start rebuilding their relationship.'

'We'll do it,' said Harry. He hung the phone up. 'Winston, we're going to be movie stars.'

Chapter Twenty-one Making up is Hard to do

It was two years later. The film had been a blockbuster and they had bought a two-bedroom flat in Manchester, overlooking the docks. The sunset and sunrise from the balcony was stunning and they often sat out there drinking wine or tea. The twins where happy that everything was going their way. They had secured a job on a sitcom in Manchester *and* been on a few dates with girls. They hadn't got anyone special but they had both broken their virginity — much to their joint delight. They had been meeting girls on the internet but also had girl fans coming up to their apartment, knocking on their door.

The post came and Winston brought it into the front room. They had lots of fan mail forwarded from the T.V. studios and from their publishing company.

'Hey,' said Harry. 'That handwriting looks familiar,' he said, picking one out from the small pile. He opened it. It was from John. 'John's written to us,' said Harry. 'Do you want me to read it out?'

'Yes please,' said Winston — he was surprised. He thought John wanted nothing to do with them.

Dear Brothers,

I've sent this letter to your publisher. I hope you get it. I've no idea where you are I hope you will ring me at the number at the top of this page. I saw your interview last year with Parkinson. Then I bought and read your autobiography 'Double Trouble'. It's clear from what you wrote, despite your mistreatment of myself and Sarah, that you still cared about us very much. I've decided to let bygones be bygones and hold out the olive branch, so to speak. The thing is, I'm getting married next month to Mary. You met her at the funeral and I'd very much like it if you both could come. The other family news you won't have heard about is Sarah had a little girl last year. You wouldn't believe who the father is. It's that snivelling little vet Rod Smith. They started seeing each other shortly after Mum's funeral. Anyway, they've moved in together. Sarah's still working at the stables; she has a nanny. They'll both be there at the wedding if you want to come.

Yours faithfully,

John Plantington

'Well I never,' said Winston.
'That's a turn up for the books, isn't it?' said Harry. 'Do you think we should go?'
'Why not?' said Winston. 'It will be fun to see everybody again.'
'We'll have to get them a present,' said Harry. 'What on Earth can we buy them? They've got everything they need already in the farmhouse.'
'I know, we could buy them a fountain for the garden,' said Winston. 'I've seen some with little cherubs pouring water out of jugs on the internet.'
'Well, you order one,' said Harry. 'I'm going to make tea.'
Just then, Harry's mobile rang. It was their agent.

'Listen darlings, how do you fancy going to L.A in America? The publishing company has decided to try to sell it in America — your autobiography — and I have managed to get you on a chat show if you interested. You know, so you can plug your book.'

'Blimey' said Harry. 'Winston, fancy a trip to America?'

'Why not?' said Winston.

It was a fine spring day. The cherry tree in the churchyard was in full blossom. The church bells peeled as people stood around gossiping. Harry and Winston stood outside the church. John saw them and came over.

'Why don't you go in and find a pew?' he said to them.

They walked in the church and sat at the back. John walked down the aisle and sat at the front of the church. Harry and Winston recognised the best man — he was one of the stable hands. He had been friends with John for years; they went to the pub together for quiz night. Sarah and Rodney walked in they walked right past the twins, not noticing them, and went to sit behind John. Then the organ started playing 'Here Comes the Bride.' Mary walked in with two young girls holding her train. She had a long white dress on and looked radiant with the flowers in her hair and red, rosy cheeks.

The service went without a hitch and everybody filed out. Harry and Winston waited for everybody to leave before Harry called a taxi on his mobile phone to take them to the reception.

When they walked into the room, everybody went silent and stared at them.
Sarah saw them come in and stood up.

'John,' she shouted. 'What are they doing here?'

'Ah, my surprise guests,' he said, running over to them.

'You are both sat over here on the top table.'

'I can't believe you invited them to your wedding — after all they did to us as kids,' gasped Sarah. 'It was bad enough when I thought they had learning difficulties, but now I know they were just winding us up...'

'Come on Sarah,' said Rod, rubbing her hand and looking at her all concerned with his puppy dog eyes. 'You don't want to get all upset — not in your condition.'

'What condition?' asked John.

'Actually, we've got a surprise,' said Rod, grinning. 'We're expecting our second child. It's a boy — we've seen its widget on the scan, haven't we darling?'

'Look Sarah,' said John. 'They're our brothers and I wanted them at our wedding. Can we not just bury the hatchet just for one day?'

'I'm sorry,' said Sarah. 'Anything you want John. It's your day, after all.'

'Yes it is my day. I'm sorry I didn't warn you. I thought I'd surprise everybody,' he said, taking a sip from his wine.

The meal came and everybody tucked in. Nobody spoke much. The atmosphere hung heavy and oppressive.

The father of the bride stood up after the meal and rattled a spoon against his glass.

'Well, I'd just like to say what a pleasure it is to be here today. To give away my daughter to John Plantington. He's a grand lad and rich as well by all accounts,' he laughed. 'Seriously, I couldn't have chosen a better man for her myself. I see this day not so much losing a daughter but gaining a bathroom. I hear you have more than one bathroom in the Plantington's farmhouse. Good job John, that's all I've got to say. Except this. Myself and mother want grandchildren, don't we dear? I've paid for the honeymoon. Now I know John didn't want to go too far away in case they needed him in the stables, so I've hired you both a villa in the south of France. Won't take you long to get home on the channel ferry in case of emergencies. Although your best man and Sarah assure me they can handle things whilst you're gone. Anyway, everybody raise your glasses to John and Mary.

'To John and Mary,' said everybody.

'I believe the best man would like a few words.'

Then the best man got up and said his speech.

'Well, me and John have been pals for some time now. He met his wife Mary when she wanted his dear departed mother's stud to mate with her friend's horse. Anyway, she must have thought our John here was a bit of a stud himself because now they're getting married. She's given him everything he ever wanted — which of course is a racehorse — one of her own horse's offspring. Mary is to move in with John and help him with the stables. I expect Mary's racehorses will be moving in as well. Sorry I couldn't think of any jokes; however, I'm very pleased for the lucky couple. They both have the same hobbies and interests, which are horses, horses and betting on horses, so they should be happy together. I know my best mate John is getting a bit fed up of rattling round in that big old farmhouse since his sister left. Anyway, raise your glasses everyone. To John and Mary.'

'To John and Mary,' said everyone, raising their

champagne glasses.

'Now I'll read the messages and cards out.

'Congratulations from Sarah, Rodney and little Dora — can't wait until little Dora has a cousin to play with.'

'Have fun and don't forget to act daft sometimes, from Harry and Winston.'

'Congratulations from everybody at Yarrow Valley Farm,' he continued.

'Sarah's named the baby after Mum,' noted Harry.

'So she has,' noted Winston.

The best man finished reading the cards and sat down.

John stood up. 'I'd just like to thank my lovely wife for agreeing to marry me. If you'll all raise your glasses to Mary.'

Everybody raised their champagne glasses.

'To Mary.'

'I'd also like to give these to my dear new mother-in-law,' he said, handing her a big bunch of flowers. 'And I've got a little thank you for the bridesmaids. I've just had some more brilliant news — Rod and Sarah are expecting their second child, so if we could toast the clever couple. To Rod and Sarah and baby....'

'James,' said Rodney. 'James, after my late father.'

Everybody raised their glasses.

'Anyway, when are you two tying the knot?' asked Mary.

'Why fix something that ain't broken?' replied Sarah. 'We're happy as we are, aren't we dear?'

'I want to get married but she keeps saying she's

fine as she is,' said Rodney.

'I'm not swapping Plantington for Smith,' she said indignantly.

'You can keep your own name these days if you want to darling,' said Rod. 'Anyway, I've got you an extra little present.' He gave Sarah a corn dolly he'd bought off a traveller. 'It's a fertility charm. I'd like to make a toast. To John and Mary; may they live long, prosper in wealth and in health, and may they bear fruit and multiply. To John and Mary.'

'To John and Mary,' said everybody, again raising their glasses.

The DJ spoke.

'Good evening everybody. Now, if the bride and groom would like to hit the dance floor for the first waltz of the evening.'

John and Mary got up and started to dance. Everybody watched.

'Those ballroom lessons they've been going to have paid off, haven't they?' said Rodney.

'Yes, they're really good,' said Sarah.

'How have you been Sarah?' asked Harry.

'Look, I'm not causing a fuss because it's Johns big day but I don't really want to make small talk with you,' said Sarah, getting flustered. 'Remember all those pony magazines you ripped up? All those toys of mine you broke? All those years of you making me and John miserable? I hated both of you and I still do. Even more so now I know there was nothing wrong with either of you.'

Harry and Winston looked at each other. Then Harry looked at his feet, shuffling them uncomfortably.

'We're sorry,' he said. 'We did care about you and John, you know.'

'I don't care — it's too late for sorry,' said Sarah.

'Come on now,' said Rod. 'You know what I said about getting upset.'

'Why did John invite them?' she said. 'He hates them as much as I do. Neither of us ever got time with Mum when we were little; she was always too busy looking after the twins. Myself and John were more or less brought up by the nanny whilst Mum ran about after the twins at their beck and Bloody call all the time.'

'Shush now,' said Rod. 'It's all water under the bridge.'

Harry and Winston were starting to feel very uncomfortable. They looked at John and Mary. They had finished dancing and now were circulating amongst the guests.

Slowly, everybody started to file onto the dance floor.

'I don't feel like dancing do you?' said Winston.

'Not really,' said Harry.

They sat quietly drinking their pints of lager until John and Mary came over at 10 o' clock.

'Mary, these are my twin brothers you heard so much about. You did meet them at Mum's funeral.'

'Pleased to meet you,' she said, shaking each of their hands.

'There is just one thing I'd like to know. I know in your book you said you took mine and Sarah's toys apart because you wanted to know how they worked, but why my homework? I was always getting in trouble in school because you ripped my homework up. When I told Mum, she would shout at me for leaving it lying around.'

'Look,' said Winston. 'I think it's time myself and Harry left.'

'No, No, stay,' said John. 'I thought you'd have been more fun than this — you are in that sitcom you star in, what is it now, *Seeing Double*? Come on, tell us all some jokes or something.'

'I think we better go,' said Harry.

'Look, we never meant to hurt you and Sarah.'

'Yes, you said in your autobiography. Still, you did hurt us, didn't you?'

'John,' said Mary. 'I think you've had too much whiskey.'

'No, no, dear, I'll be quiet now,' he said, staggering slightly. 'Have you seen what they bought us? That huge, tasteless water fountain for the back garden. I thought they'd have bought us his and her Rolex watches or something, especially with their money.'

'Come on,' said Harry, 'we're leaving.'

They virtually ran out of the reception, tears streaming down their faces and went to the pub across the road to phone a taxi.

'I thought John and Sarah were going to make up with us,' sobbed Winston.

'I thought it was too much to ask to be part of a family again,' said Harry, blowing his nose. 'We'll never get to know our nieces and nephews, will we?'

'No!' said Winston. 'I wonder where Rod and Sarah's baby is?

'Probably left her with the nanny.'

The taxi turned up, they went back to their flat, and both sobbed themselves to sleep.

Chapter Twenty-Two From Mancs to L.A

The twins sat under the hot studio lights of the filming studio in L.A. Their flight over had been uneventful.

David the interviewer spoke.

'I've read your autobiography, *Double Trouble*. I hear there's a film coming out. Tell me, do your brother and sister still resent you for all the tricks and pranks you played on them?'

'Yes they do,' said Harry. 'They'll never forgive us.'

'We were young and stupid,' added Winston. 'We love our family, it's a great source of distress to us that John and Sarah don't want anything to do with us anymore.'

'Yes,' continued Harry. 'Our sister Sarah has a baby and is expecting another one. We'll never get to know our nieces and nephews.'

'What started you off behaving like this in the first place? I mean, what was the catalyst?' asked David.

'Well, when baby Sarah was first born and started taking away our mother's attention, we decided we didn't need anybody but each other,' explained Harry.

'Yes, but at the same time we were jealous of the other two children and any attention our dear departed mother gave to them.'

'But you regret it now, treating your brother and sister so badly?'

'Yes we do. We want so much to be a part of their life — to be a part of a family again,' said Harry.

'Yes, we regretted it as soon as we were sent to live on the supported housing scheme. We missed all our family so much.' Winston leaned forward. 'We wished so much we had acted normal and helped out with the chores and helped in the stables like John and Sarah so we could both be part of our family.'

'You said in the book your mum came back to you as a ghost after she died. Do you really expect anybody to believe that?'

'It could have been some strange, shared dream I suppose,' offered Winston. 'All I know is that we both saw her.'

'And this led you to leave in the middle of the night and go to Blackpool. What made you go into acting?'

'Well, we've been acting daft all our lives,' said Harry.

'Ladies and gentlemen, The Stargazey twins,' said David.

There was a round of applause.

Later, back in their hotel room, they had opened a bottle of wine when there was a knock on the door. Winston opened it. There stood a pair of brown-eyed, beautiful identical twins.

'Yes?' enquired Winston.

The twins stared at each other and giggled.

'We're great fans of yours,' said one.

'Yes, can we have your autograph?' said the other.

'Come in,' said Winston. 'Would you like some wine?'

'Yes please,' said the girls, giggling uncontrollably.

'So, what're your names?' asked Winston.

'My name's Gloria and this is Isobel,' said one of

the ladies.

Harry put some romantic music on his CD player and soon they were all up dancing. Both of the twins had been instantly attracted to the girls. They drank more wine.

'So, what do you do?' Harry asked the girls.

'We're both supermarket checkout girls,' replied Gloria.

'That sounds interesting,' said Winston.

'Stop humouring us,' said Isobel. 'It's a boring, dead-end job I wished we'd paid more attention at school instead of messing about.'

'I know the feeling,' said Winston.

All of a sudden, Harry became overcome with emotion.

'Will you both marry us?' he said, taking it for granted that Winston would be feeling the same way as him.

'Yes,' squealed the girls with delight.

The night wore on and they ended up making sweet love to the girls on their respective beds. Harry and Winston had been feeling so depressed, but now they were on top of the world as they each brought their girlfriend to orgasm, pumping their passion inside them. Then all four of them fell into a blissful sleep.

They awoke in the morning and Harry called room service for breakfast. It came up with four full English breakfasts and they all ate heartily.

'Listen,' said Harry. 'We're booked on a plane back to England this afternoon; can we have your telephone numbers and email addresses?'

'Certainly,' said Gloria. 'You will ring, won't you?'

'Try stopping us,' said Winston.

'I thought you'd have stayed a few days,' said Gloria.

'We have to get back. We're filming *Seeing Double*,' said Harry.

'Yes, but we can come back and see you after the end of the series,' said Winston.

'How do you fancy coming to live in England?' asked Harry.

'Oh, I don't know, it's a long way off,' said Gloria.

'Yes,' said Isobel. 'It's a bit too far away from our mum.'

'I wonder if we can get work over here?' said Harry. 'There's no one keeping us in England.'

'We'll have to see,' said Winston.

The boys kissed a girl each and the girls left.

'Bye,' they said shyly. They couldn't believe they'd just spent the night with the Stargazey twins and they'd asked for their hands in marriage.

'Do you really think they'll ring us?' Gloria asked her sister.

'I don't know,' replied Isobel.

Later that afternoon, Harry and Winston were on the plane back to England. They sat sipping a whiskey each as they ate their in-flight meal.

Suddenly, the pilot's voice came over the tannoy.

'Can everybody fasten their seatbelts please? One of the engines is failing.'

A woman behind them started screaming.

'How can we fasten our seatbelts with the trays down?' asked Winston.

'Don't worry,' said Harry. 'It'll be all right.'

Just then, the plane started to nosedive and

everybody started to scream. Food and drink off people's seats flew everywhere. Harry and Winston went flying out of their seats. Then everything went blank.

They awoke on a dual carriageway, somewhere in America. The screaming had stopped. Bits of aircraft where strewn all over the place. Some cars had been hit by bits of flying debris. All of a sudden, they heard a voice behind them.

'My beautiful boys. Shame they'll never get married.'

They looked behind them.

'Mum!' they both cried.

'Come with me,' she said, and she walked over the road into the field and the twins followed. There on the grass lay their own dead bodies.

'Are we dead?' asked Winston.

'Yes,' said Mum. 'I'm afraid your time's up.'

'But we can't be — we were going to move to L.A and get married, and have children.'

'I'm afraid not,' said Mum. 'When your time's up, your time's up. I've come to get you to take you to the other side.' She held out her hands and the twins took one each.

'One thing,' said Harry. 'Are you proud of us?'

'Of course,' said Mum, smiling. 'I knew you'd snap out of it one day, make something of yourselves. Come now, Dad and Grandma and everybody is waiting for you on the other side. Come with me towards the light.'

The twins looked behind Mother — there was a tunnel of light. They walked into it and then, in a flash, they were gone.

ACTING DAFT

ACTING DAFT

ACTING DAFT

ACTING DAFT

ACTING DAFT

Printed in the United Kingdom by
Lightning Source UK Ltd., Milton Keynes
137353UK00001B/73-81/P

9 781847 477286